4/04

PRAISE FOR

ANOTHER RIVER, ANOTHER TOWN

"A taut, insightful story told by a thoughtful soldier. It's as fine a combat memoir as you're likely to encounter."

—Flint, Michigan, *Journal*

"Irwin has produced a straightforward account of his weeks in the front lines of the European Theater, without self-analysis, without attempting to impart any 'message' beyond the horror demonstrated by events themselves."

—*St. Petersburg Times*

"A well-written and easily read story that is remembered from a perspective rarely told."

—Williamsport, Pennsylvania, *Sun-Gazette*

"Not only a first-person history lesson . . . [but] a deeply psychological look at war and death through a teenager's eyes. You'll be hooked from the very first page."

—Lancaster, Pennsylvania, *New Era*

JOHN P. IRWIN was born in Norristown, Pennsylvania, in 1926 and enlisted in the army in August 1944. He was honorably discharged in July 1946 and went on to Ursinus College in 1952, eventually earning his Ph.D. in philosophy from Syracuse University. He taught philosophy at Lock Haven University from 1964 to his retirement in 1990. He lives in Lock Haven, Pennsylvania.

ANOTHER RIVER,
ANOTHER TOWN

JOHN P. IRWIN

ANOTHER RIVER, ANOTHER TOWN

A TEENAGE TANK
GUNNER COMES OF AGE
IN COMBAT—1945

RANDOM HOUSE TRADE PAPERBACKS
NEW YORK

2003 Random House Trade Paperback Edition

Copyright © 2002 by John P. Irwin

This work was originally published in hardcover by Random House, Inc., in 2002.

Library of Congress Cataloging-in-Publication Data
Irwin, John P.
Another river, another town: a teenage tank gunner comes
of age in combat—1945 / John P. Irwin.
p.   cm.
ISBN 0-375-75963-8
1. Irwin, John P., 1926–   2. World War, 1939–1945—Personal narratives,
American.   3. World War, 1939–1945—Campaigns—Germany.
4. Soldiers—United States—Biography.   5. World War, 1939–1945—
Tank warfare.   I. Title.
D811.I77 A3   2002   940.54'8173—dc21   2001048482

Printed in the United States of America
Random House website address: www.atrandom.com
2 4 6 8 9 7 5 3 1

Book design by J. K. Lambert

TO THE MEN OF SPEARHEAD

1944-1945

FOREWORD

The Second World War was the last declared war the United States fought in the twentieth century. Like its predecessor of 1914–18, in which patriotism brought the nation together in a very short time, this war also enlisted the aid of millions of young men and women in military and support services, and drew tight the cord of national unity. It was, nevertheless, a war, and in all wars young combatants interrupt their lives to learn the arts of killing and destruction and survival. And those who succeed in the last of these are forever burdened with the memories of the first two.

The men of the military services were treated like heroes for going to war and even more like heroes when they returned victoriously. But they were, in reality, civilians in uniform. The services were not made up of professionals, and the great majority had had no intention of entering a military career. But what they lacked in regimental polish they made up for in determination, endurance, ingenuity, and indomitable morale. And fundamental to that morale was the special sense of humor they possessed, one that emerged even in the darkest moments of combat. The war was hardly funny, but it did provide a setting for its own strange kind of humor.

This is a personal story, an account of an adolescent wanna-be adult whose brief struggle with the war coincided with his wretched struggle with his developing sexual maleness. Somehow, war and testosterone mix well—though together they do not produce happiness.

ACKNOWLEDGMENTS

I am indebted to the official record of the 3rd Armored Division, Spearhead in the West, *for certain details such as specific dates, several place names, and other information that had faded from my memory over the years.*

I wish to acknowledge the help and encouragement of my editor, Bob Loomis, whose first critique of the manuscript put me on the right track.

CONTENTS

ANOTHER RIVER,

ANOTHER TOWN

CHAPTER 1

THE EDUCATION OF
A HERO

The German breakthrough in the Ardennes forest in France in December of 1944 and January of 1945 created a "bulge" extending into Allied positions. In the ensuing battle, one of the most horrendous and costly conflicts in the European theater in World War II—the Battle of the Bulge—the Allies lost enormous quantities of equipment, men, and supplies. The need to pursue the now retreating Germans required massive replacements of equipment and, especially, men. There was no way the war could continue without them.

At that very moment, I was being prepared—along with tens of thousands of other GIs—to help supply the need. I had found my heroic destiny in armored warfare, and my training at Fort Knox, Kentucky, resulted in my qualifying best as a "medium tank gunner." I was a normal teenager, just eighteen, naïve, ignorant, fully absorbed in myself, and quite certain that I knew all I needed to know about the world—in fact, next to nothing—and was invulnerable to such subtleties as death and destruction. My education about the war was pretty much limited to the *Why We Fight* indoctrination films we were required to watch in basic training. Those films filled me with adolescent hostility toward Adolf Hitler and his armies, whose satanic goal, we were assured, was to conquer the world and make slaves of us all.

I was a griping-good soldier and wanted more than anything to go to Germany, find Hitler, and relieve the world of that monster once and for all. Not all the trainees I associated with shared my zeal; in fact, lots of guys were finding ingenious ways to avoid shipping out to the ETO (European Theater of Operations). Most of them were draftees. I, on the other hand, had enlisted, primarily to avoid finishing high school, which I detested. Surely war was preferable to high school!

I had as good a training at Fort Knox as nineteen weeks (including two weeks of gunnery school) would permit, and by the time I arrived in Europe, I had received the corporal stripes that went with being a gunner. I had the romantic idea that in some sense war was glorious. But the devastation I saw in France, Belgium, and Germany was so nearly total in places that my illusions began to fade. A lot of boys became men in those first days, though some of us held on to our heroic fantasies, our dramatic dreams of doing great things in battle. We rode across France and Belgium in "40-and-8s" of World War I vintage and ended up in the tangle of destruction in Germany called Stolberg.

At Stolberg we were detained in a replacement depot (or "repple-depple") situated in a former chain factory. Our private quarters consisted of whatever vacant spots we could find on the filthy floor. The air was choked with the smoke of burning shoe impregnate, which was considered more valuable as a source of heat than as protection of shoes and feet against mustard gas. And everywhere, of course, were the countless barracks bags and other equipment the men were responsible for. I saw no glory here! But it was here that we were, without our knowledge or consent, assigned to various line outfits, our combat units. I did not know what my assignment would be when we finally convoyed out of Stolberg into the vast unknown of combat war-fare. I still remember the tingle of excitement I felt as we trav-eled across the wreckage-strewn countryside. The carcasses of tanks, trucks, half-tracks, even planes, gave us some impression of what lay ahead for us.

One of the remarkable things about combat life is the almost total and perpetual blindness of individual soldiers when it comes to the matters that most immediately affect them. We never knew what was going on, where we were going, what we would be doing, or, of course, what the outcome would be. We thought we knew, because there was always an abundance of rumors, all said to be gleaned from the most authoritative sources. Next to mail and food, rumors are the lifeblood of military existence. And incredible as it may seem, though the rumors are generally proven either false or exaggerated, soldiers never lose faith in them. They are, after all, the only show in town when it comes to information.

Our small convoy traveled several hours before coming to a fairly extensive wasteland of frozen mud covered with many hun-dreds of military vehicles, most of them armored. To my left I noticed a small column of Sherman tanks on what was presum-ably a roadway. Around the area men were everywhere, walking, sitting on their bags, leaning on vehicles, and, invariably, smoking. The one thing more ubiquitous than rumor-mongering in this army was cigarette smoking. The ten or twenty GIs in the entire European theater who did not smoke were forever on the defensive to explain what their problem was. Besides the hundreds of tanks and half-tracks, there were large numbers of armored cars, trucks, peeps (later known as "jeeps"), command cars, and the like.

We dismounted from our trucks, lit up our cigarettes, and put our hands in our pockets. It was very cold. Our little convoy had been under the direction of a second lieutenant, and he had walked away somewhere, cigarette in mouth, hands in pockets, looking for someone to report to. The going rumor was that we had been assigned to the 3rd Armored Division with the First Army—a rumor that for once turned out to be correct. The information meant next to nothing to me, since I knew nothing about army units. Yet, for some reason I felt good about it. Now I had an identity, a home plate, so to speak, an address I could call my own. All I wanted now was to move out of this mudhole and on to my new unit.

There was a great deal of urgency in that open air reppledepple. The command here wanted to move us out just as urgently as most of us wanted to go, and our wish was about to be granted. The tanks lined up on the roadway were waiting for us to take them up to the assigned unit. One tank, however, stood off the roadway, apart from the others, undergoing some sort of maintenance. At the sound of a whistle we were lined up, counted off in fours, and directed to the various tanks. As it happened, three other guys and myself were assigned to the stray tank not in the column. As we stood dumbly by the tank, a captain came over to us, and, seeing my corporal stripes, he spoke to me.

"I need someone in charge here. You seem to be the ranking person, Corporal, so that will be you. Who's a driver?"

A long moment dragged by. Finally a reluctant voice with a Virginia drawl said, "Uh, Ah guess that would be me."

"Okay. You other two will go along for the ride. I'm Captain Harkin, and I'm in command of this convoy until we get to the 33rd Armored Regiment."

"Sir?" I ventured.

"What is it?" he asked briskly.

"I thought we were going to the 3rd Armored Division."

"Damn it, you are," he snapped, "at least you are as soon as these mechanics say your tank is ready to roll. The rest of us are going to take advantage of what daylight is left and move out. You'll be on your way to catch up to us within twenty or thirty minutes. But remember. This is hostile country. It hasn't been completely cleared of the enemy. The SS may be anywhere around here waiting for a chance to create diversions. *No lights!* Get it? N-O-N-E. Even a lit cigarette outside your tank could draw fire from God knows where. You'll be given driving instructions before you leave."

He pulled his cigarette from his mouth and stomped it into the mud.

"Any questions?" he asked.

I asked the obvious one. "Will we have to shoot?"

"I hope not," he said. "You certainly won't be shooting that cannon, for God's sake. Any other questions?"

After Captain Harkin left, we stood in a silent clump a short distance from our tank, watching the maintenance crew working on it.

"You a good driver?" I asked the Virginian, whose name turned out to be Dennis Graver.

"Ah'm qualified." He shuddered. "Ah sure don' wanna stan' around here long, though."

The other two were quiet. One—Eddie Evangelini—was no older than I and looked just as underage. "I never expected this kind of duty when I got drafted," he whimpered. Our fourth member said very little, though he wore a funny smile, as though he knew something we didn't. I wasn't sure I liked him. He said his name was Hominy. Har-dee-har-har, I thought, so call me Grits!

It was forty-five minutes before our tank was ready to roll. Graver got directions from a lieutenant, who assured him he would have no trouble. Just stay on the road. When we get to a small town, the rest of the convoy will be waiting for us. But remember: NO LIGHTS!

No lights, and a cold winter dusk had settled in, making the road virtually invisible. To add to these troubles, a haze of dust hung in the frigid air from the tank convoy that had passed on ahead. Dust! Sherman tanks were technology's answer to clean air. They were extremely efficient dust machines. Take one road caked with winter mud, drive a Sherman tank over it, listen to the clanking, crunching, and shrieking as the heavy treads grind the frozen mud to powder, and enjoy the spectacle of tremendous clouds of dust being blown into the air by the downward blast of the rear exhaust. And they said, *"No lights!"* From my perspective, lights wouldn't have made a particle of difference.

Graver was obviously in the grip of terror. The mention of SS troopers had fired his brain. From that moment on he was a changed man. He had come under the control of a higher power called FEAR. His foot pressed that Sherman accelerator flat to the floor of the tank. It was never clear, at any given moment, whether or not we were on the road at all—not that it mattered that much to Graver. I could hear Evangelini utter a "Holy shit!" from the depths of the tank, but Hominy just stood on the back deck of the tank nonchalantly, as though it didn't matter one way or another.

But it did matter. Graver could not see more than twenty yards before him, and he had those rolling thirty-five tons moving at about forty-five miles an hour. The impact of one tank upon another at that speed invariably produces effects no one would wish for. In the present case—unknown (and invisible) to us—the convoy that preceded us had stopped at an intersection in the road to take bearings. When our tank rammed full speed into the last tank in the convoy, Hominy completed a beautiful loft over our tank turret onto the back deck of the tank we had rammed. I suppose it would have been fun to watch, but it was no fun when Captain Harkin showed up to inspect the damage.

"I'll be a mother—" he began, shaking his head incredulously. "This *has* to be history in the making!" He examined what was left of the shattered drive sprocket on our tank and the separated tread lying twisted in the road. "Jesus Christ! What the hell were you trying to do?" he croaked at no one in particular. Graver sat with a dazed look in the driver's hatch, not entirely sure what had gone wrong. Evangelini was buried somewhere in the inner sanctum of the tank hull, apparently not even breathing. I stood by Captain Harkin shaking my head in sync with his, trying to make the point that those of us in command often have to put up with some pretty stupid things.

"What's your name, Corporal?"

"Irwin, sir. Corporal John P. Irwin."

"Didn't you notice how fast this son of a bitch was moving?"

"Well, yes, sir, I thought it was kind of fast," I offered defensively.

"No, Corporal. It wasn't *kind of* fast. It was very, *very* fast. It was the bloody fastest fucking tank driving I've seen in this war. I've been around this war awhile, and I didn't know tanks could go that fast."

"What do you think we should do, sir?" I ventured.

The captain cast a scowl my way and walked over to his peep. He radioed the maintenance people in the rear. A few minutes later he came back.

"Bad luck! No one can do anything for you before tomorrow afternoon. The rear has its own problems. Your trapeze man got himself hurt. No telling how bad. We're taking him with us. You three will have to stand guard right here in the middle of this intersection until the maintenance people can get to you. And when I say stand guard, I mean just that. See these woods all around here?" He circled his arm at the nearby hills. "They're swarming with fucking SS just squirming to shoot your asses off."

I was sorry Graver had to hear that remark. His head disappeared down the driver's hatch, just like a turtle retreating into its shell. The hatch closed, and I could hear it latch. No one was going to shoot *his* ass off! From the still-open turret hatch I could hear repetitive pleas to the Mother of God to have mercy and forgive and protect this unworthy servant.

As the convoy of tanks roared off into the night, I listened to the fading echoes. Somehow, this was not at all what I had expected of combat. It wasn't clear what I did expect, but this surely was not it. For the first time I became aware that our tank was positioned in the middle of an intersection, not more than twenty feet from a house. In fact, I could just make out that there were other houses in the area, though I saw no lights and no signs of living beings. It was going to be a lonely vigil indeed.

My only companion during that excruciatingly long night was my "grease gun," a strange little collapsible submachine gun that fired fifteen rounds of .45-caliber bullets per clip with forty-five percent accuracy up to twenty-five yards. I often wondered if I could hit the hull of a tank from the inside with one of these babies. Nevertheless, one thing was certain: no one was going to get me to sit inside that iron coffin in a situation like this. I'd seen lots of war movies, and I knew all about how the Krauts would open hatches and throw hand grenades inside tanks. So I chose to sit on the steps of the nearest house, on guard, with my trusty grease gun cradled in my arms. Which I did all night long!

Wherever the SS troops were, they never showed themselves to me that night. And in the morning I sat, cold and groggy, on the steps of the house, still cradling my first and only line of defense in my arms and smoking a cigarette. There was no sign of life about our tank. My two stalwart companions were still too terrified to venture outside, not even for necessary activities. I could only imagine the condition of things inside, and I was glad for the fresh air.

The tank was stocked with water and rations, so we did not

starve or die of thirst before the maintenance people showed up late in the afternoon. The water cans were blocked with ice, but we managed to melt that without setting Germany on fire. The three of us stood around the three of them, who were having problems replacing our drive sprocket.

"Never seen anything like this," complained the staff sergeant in charge. "Y'all musta put lily grease on them tracks to slide that hard."

"Oh, we didn't slide," explained Graver. "Ah never even put on the brakes—never saw a thing in front of me. It was just *slammo!*"

"Shit! You boys are luckier'n hell you wasn't killed," came a voice from under the tank. "When we git this thing runnin' fer ya, y'all better take real good care of it, 'cause we ain't got no more spare sprockets layin' around."

It took more than an hour and a half for the repair team to complete the task, and I was getting very nervous as I watched the sun disappear behind the trees.

"You guys got any idea what we do now?" I asked, trying not to look too stupid.

The lanky redheaded sergeant raised up to his full six-foot-three frame and looked down at me, wiping his greasy hands on a greasy rag and grinning as he did so.

"My first word to y'all is keep yer distance from that chicken-shit captain. He chews nails and spits carpet tacks an' don't care who steps on 'em. He has a short temper and a long memory."

"Yeah, but . . . well . . . where are we supposed to go now?" I whimpered. "The captain never gave us any directions."

A small private appeared from behind the tank, adjusting his helmet liner and then blowing on his hands.

"You boys lost?" he cackled gleefully. "Guess you gone hafta just wander around till you run out of gas."

I pretended not to take offense and held out my pack of cigarettes to the trio.

"Look," I pleaded as they helped themselves to my cigarettes, "we're fresh from the States and we're s'posed to take this tank to the 33rd Armored Regiment. But we don't know anything about these roads. Don't any of you guys . . ."

"Don't piss your pants!" exclaimed the redhead. "Y'all ain't got no problem if ya just follow my directions."

"Graver!" I called. "C'mere! Get these instructions!"

The two of us listened carefully, never thinking to write anything down, not that we had anything to write with. After the short briefing, we thanked the trio, who were already driving away in their truck. We mounted our tank, Graver driving, and roared, clanked, and squealed noisily down the road. The instructions were simple enough, though vaguer than I would have liked. "Several kilometers" did not register anything specific with me. I wasn't really sure how far a kilometer was. I hoped Graver had a better idea, but he didn't.

It was getting very dark. In fact it got so dark that it became impossible to see the road at all. Graver had the tank creeping. Finally, I got down from the turret and walked in front of the tank so Graver could stay on the road. I was able to see the edge of the road—just. But what a slow process it became! How long we traveled this way is hard to estimate. It seemed like hours—and it probably was. Eventually, however, we came to an intersection where we were faced with a choice of three directions. Graver and I argued over what we each believed the instructions had been. I was unsure of my own interpretation, but I was willing to follow my instincts. Graver, on the other hand, was adamant in his belief that we were to take the right fork. So, he being the driver, right it was.

Travel along this new road was not much better than on the previous one. It was, at least, possible for me to ride instead of walk, but the whole time we rode, I worried about where we were headed and what we might run into. A Sherman tank does not slip quietly along the way, and I was sure that somewhere in that impenetrable darkness were enemy forces focusing in on the sound of our metal monster with their legendary "88s." Here was a superversatile cannon with such muzzle velocity that even without armor-piercing ammo it could send a shot in one side and out the other of a Sherman. I suddenly felt extremely vulnerable sitting on the right sponson of the tank. I had seen only a dormant example of an 88 at Fort Knox and had never even heard one fire. And I did not desire that pleasure at this time.

We had been driving for more than half an hour before I realized that we were passing houses, all of them totally dark. I signaled to Graver to stop the tank. I had no idea what was going on with Evangelini; he was probably curled up in a fetal position somewhere in the depths of the tank. I signaled to cut the engine. When nothing but the ringing in my ears could be heard, I ventured down from the tank for a look-see. We had obviously entered a town. If we were lucky, it was the town where we were to join the rest of the convoy.

"Wait here," I murmured to Graver. "I'll check things out, see if I can find the CP."

Graver said nothing. He just did his turtle thing and disappeared under the locking hatch. I walked cautiously down the road until I came to a sidewalk. I felt relief. Even more when I detected the shadowy shapes of tanks along the street. Every house was in total darkness, not a sound, not a sight, until I came to one house from which a thin sliver of light fell on the ground. Heavy curtains were slightly open on the window, so I surmised that here was the CP—the command post—and prepared myself for another interview with the infamous Captain Harkin. I hoped that this time things would go a bit more amicably.

I slipped up to the parted curtains and peered in. The hair on the nape of my neck crawled as I viewed a small cluster of German officers sitting in various attitudes around a makeshift command center. The feeling of shock was surpassed only by the sinking sense of despair I felt as the horrible realization of my situation locked me in its tentacles. Oh God! I thought, Germans! I haven't even had a chance to fire a cannon, let alone kill Hitler. And now I'm about to become a prisoner of war! Gotta get outta here. What I had failed to notice in the darkness was that the tanks along the street were German panzers.

As I hurried back to the tank, I harbored the incredibly futile hope that perhaps somehow our presence had escaped the Germans' notice. Maybe—just maybe—we could start up our tank and slip smoothly (if not quietly) away and take our chances elsewhere. All my glorious fantasies of heroism and medals had suddenly shattered into infinitesimal shards of nonsense. Reality was pressed all the more on me when, upon arrival back at the tank, I saw a German soldier just a few feet away pointing a gun directly at a spot between my two bleary eyes.

"You are American?" he asked.

I swallowed something undetectable in my throat, put my hands upon my head, and replied, in my best German, "Ja."

"Ach! Sie sprechen Deutsch!" he exclaimed and proceeded to assemble a string of hopelessly unintelligible syllables.

"No," I muttered. "I sprechen English."

"Es macht nicht," he said. In a proud, supercilious tone he went on, "I speak excellent English."

I stood and stared at him. A young guy, somewhere around my age, some sort of noncom, not really very threatening. I waited.

"You are to come mit me to Colonel Schnidell at our head-quarterses. Please do not try to escape from me or I will be re-quired to shooting you in the bottom of your pantses."

He seemed like a nice enough guy—a little stupid, but a nice guy. Of course, I wasn't considering the fact that he spoke English and I spoke no German. He walked beside me, swinging his rifle back and forth, the barrel occasionally hitting the sidewalk, producing tiny sparks, while attempting to explain to me that I was his gallant foe and that he was hoping I could be of help to "his people." I hadn't the foggiest notion what he was talking about, but I praised the Almighty that he had not shot me be-tween the eyes.

"That's not good for your gun," I ventured, as he continued to swing the weapon back and forth.

"Gun?" he said. "This gun—it has no . . . no . . ."

"Bullets?" I offered.

"Nein. It has bullets, but no shooter thing. It is—how do you say it in English—no good."

"Kaput?" I offered, exhausting my German vocabulary.

He seemed impressed. "Ja—yes. Kaput."

So, I followed the kaput-rifle-swinging enemy noncom into the enemy headquarters with the slightly open curtains and waited for the introductions. The officer in charge—a colonel, presumably—spoke in quiet German to the young non-com, looking at me the whole time. He made no impassioned speech, something I thought all Nazis did under such circumstances.

When he was finished, the soldier spoke to me.

"My Kommandant wishes you to be at ease and have no fear. No one wishes to harm you. We no longer consider ourselves combatants. We have been left behind by the retreating German forces to create a diversion and slow the Americans down. We have a small force of a little over one hundred mens. We have no benzene for our tanks. We do not wish to resist. My Kommandant wishes to surrender his forces to the American army."

He paused and looked at his commander. The latter spoke a few words, and he continued. "My Kommandant cannot surrender to someone of your lowly rank, and he wishes for you tanks people to take him to your headquarterses so he can surrender in the . . . uh . . ."

"Proper way?" I ventured.

"Ja! Yes. Proper way."

It was all coming slowly into focus for me. I was not to be the prisoner after all—*they* were. I was to be the captor. I was to bring in a whole bunch of German prisoners of war, sort of like Sergeant York. The bold fantasies returned with greater bravado than before. I pulled myself up to my full five feet five and a half inches and nodded dramatically. I then remembered that I had not the slightest idea where my headquarters were. I suddenly crumpled in embarrassment. All eyes were on me.

"Er, tell your commander that I, uh, think his idea is a good one." I hesitated. How can I be a hero if I don't even know where I am? I folded. "I'm sorry. Tell your commander that I haven't any idea where my unit is. Actually—we're lost." These last words trailed off with shame, and I looked downward at my boots.

There was no sense of amusement or dismay among the Germans. The Kommandant motioned for me to come over to the map on the rickety table he was standing by. He pointed out the spot on the map where we were at present and traced the path we would have to follow to arrive at the small town of Mengendorf, where the Americans were located. I marveled at this astonishing piece of intelligence and gained an instant admiration for the German military mind. And I felt very grateful.

Tomorrow, I was told, the contingent of German troops would ride in two trucks. The four officers, of course, would ride in the command car. Our tank would lead. Throughout the night the Germans busied themselves siphoning what benzene they could from the panzers to fuel their trucks. Equipment had to be packed, weapons destroyed, and most records were burned.

I tried to explain our situation to Graver and Evangelini, but they were sure it was a Nazi trick of some sort. I didn't much care what Evangelini thought, but I needed Graver to drive. Not that I couldn't have done it myself, but I would rather be up on the turret, where a commander should be, as we arrived at our destination.

"Graver," I argued, "we don't have a choice. If we don't do what they say, they'll just shoot us and let our bodies rot. But if we do, we'll be able to get to our outfit like heroes."

Graver was not stupid. He saw the logic and finally agreed to drive. Anything was better than cringing in that freeze box just waiting for some fate to destroy him.

I felt exhausted and descended into a profound snore-a-thon, sitting in the gunner's seat in the turret. A banging on the sponson jarred me back from Somnalia, where I didn't even have a decent dream. It was time to leave. The German vehicles were already lined up; it was now our time for glory. And what a triumphant feeling it was as we revved up our tank and began our heroic trek to the American side. The young German noncom sat on the turret with me, his finger placed permanently on the ragged map he had been given to guide us. We talked very little, and what conversation we had was against great odds—the roar of the engine and his odd German-English. The thing he enjoyed most about the arrangement was the enviable chance to smoke an American cigarette.

The distance we were to travel, I had been informed, was about sixty or so kilometers. It took nearly four hours, however, due to the necessary stops for physical relief and occasional repair on the trucks. It turned out to be more grueling than I had imagined. But as we finally approached Mengendorf, I felt a surge of warmth and grandness come over me. I tried not to show any sign of smugness or pride. I was, after all, just an ordinary GI doing what I had been sent over to do.

The stucco houses along the street were small and spaced very close together. American tanks were parked in a mud field not far down the street, and peeps and trucks and the like were parked along the road. We were, of course, the central focus of interest to the GIs along the way. To a man, they stopped whatever they were doing and stared at our bedraggled procession making its way down the street. There is no way to describe my personal sense of the historic at that moment. It was now time to cash in my chips and report to the officer in charge.

I signaled for Graver to stop, holding my hand up for the Germans to follow suit, and called to a GI.

"Hey, soldier, can you tell me where the CP is?"

I got a funny look from the dumpy PFC.

"You sure you want to go there?" he asked.

"Of course! I have to. Where is it?"

He gave me a huge grin and pointed down the street.

"Can you see that house with the regimental flag hangin' out?"

"Yeah," I called.

"That's it!"

"Thanks," I yelled as I signaled to Graver to rev up.

"Pleasure's all mine," he saluted. "*All* mine."

We drove the short distance down the street and stopped in front of the command post. I nodded toward the German colonel and gestured to wait where they were. With a strong sense of my duty, I jumped down from the tank and marched myself—in my best military fashion—right up to the door. I knocked. Eventually a voice yelled, "It's not locked!"

Inside, at a small kitchen table, sat a familiar figure. Captain Harkin was hunched over it, apparently working on reports. I snapped to attention and saluted. The salute was not returned, nor did the captain look up.

"Corporal John P. Irwin, 13197627, reporting, sir."

Without raising his eyes from his work, the captain said, "Those your prisoners out there?"

"Yes sir!" I replied, struggling to contain myself.

"That's nice," he murmured quietly. He paused, then asked, "Now what exactly do you propose to do with them?"

"Sir?" I asked.

"Well, Corporal," he continued in a restrained tone, looking up at me, "they *are* your prisoners, aren't they? You captured them, didn't you? So you should have the privilege of disposing of them. I suggest you go out and do it now—but be back here in fifteen minutes. I plan to have a roll call."

"Sir?" I gasped incredulously. "I . . . don't understand . . . what I'm supposed to do."

I watched and waited as he deliberately let what seemed like hours pass. Finally, he rose from his chair, leaned forward, bracing himself with both hands on the table, and glared at me with a fury such as I had last seen on my father's face when I flunked eleventh grade.

I choose to omit here the captain's ensuing tour de force of specialized military vernacular, which enlarged my own vocabulary of profane utterances and which contained references to unseemly behavior of sons toward their mothers. The tirade lasted most of the afternoon, or so it seemed, during which time I gradually came to realize that I was being demoted from Sergeant York to "Sad Sack," from national hero to inept civilian bumbler who just happened to be in uniform.

The point behind all this outrage was that the captain, in close contact with regimental headquarters some miles ahead, had carefully and deliberately guided the convoy around the town where I had "captured" my prisoners. Army intelligence knew they were there and suspected that they wanted to surrender. However, there were no holding facilities within a hundred miles, so prisoners at this juncture would only slow down the movement of the needed replacements.

I stood before the captain, a shivering adolescent devoid of any defense to offer other than a feeble, "It was a mistake, sir. We didn't know."

Captain Harkin, his head of steam depleted, softened his look for a moment.

"I have to get in touch with headquarters. I've already informed them of this bit of . . . of bad luck. Gotta find out what's being done. You're excused, Corporal." Then, as I started toward the door, he added, "Corporal!" I hesitated. "It's okay. You're not in trouble. Just get the hell outta my sight and try to learn the facts of life."

I was totally numb as I stepped out of the house. A cluster of GIs all started talking to me at the same time. The sense seemed to be one of incredulity that I had survived the interview, free to mess up another time. To my surprise, MPs were leading the Germans away to be confined in a temporary holding compound until more permanent arrangements could be made. One of them was directing Graver to move the tank to the mud field with the other tanks. I had no idea where the MPs came from, nor did I care at this point. All I wanted to do was crawl into the turret of that heartless Sherman tank and pretend the whole episode never happened. I noticed Evangelini sleeping on the turret floor and thought, for him it never did happen. Some guys are just dumb lucky. But at the moment I didn't feel like one of them.

CHAPTER 2

FIRST LESSONS

At eighteen I was experiencing the tenuous nature of existence in a war zone, where life is often tragic and death a release. Of course, I didn't really believe in a *personal* death. What eighteen-year-old does? Others die. That's one of the laws of death. "Everybody dies" means everybody *else* dies. Who can conceive of his own nonexistence?—if that's what death is. That's why religion is so popular, with its promise of immortality, some sort of transcendence of death, a way to stand up against the fear that eventually it will all be over, actually and completely over. And I, who did not really believe in death, was able to fall back on the religious promise I had been indoctrinated with, namely, that all my sins had been forgiven and there is thus no end to life—if not in the here then in the hereafter. I refused to think about the "hereafter," because I wanted the here-and-now to go on and on no matter what happened.

At eighteen the most important part of life is sex, whether or not you are having it. All the male pressures to become a hero or to achieve some illusion of greatness are but the ploys of those miserable sex hormones in a boy—a guy—that manipulate him ever to think of sex, or some substitute for sex. But there is a terrible conflict between this drive for sex and the "beautiful hope of salvation" that had dominated my adolescent years so far. The army was not like home, where a dear and loving mother cherished virtue beyond all else, and where a grabby religion had imposed its ultra-narrow conception of what "salvation" requires of a person.

The unit I had been assigned to, Company I, 33rd Armored Regiment, 3rd Armored Division, First U.S. Army, had been nearly wiped out in the Battle of the Bulge and was virtually a brand-new company. Fully two-thirds of the company were fresh recruits from the States, wholly untested by the fiery blasts of battle and quite bewildered by most of what they saw. The replacements had been trickling in for the past month or so. It soon became clear to the replacements that no training possible could ever prepare a person for the unholy guts of daily combat. It is one thing to learn the lessons of military training, but something completely different to experience the atmosphere of war. Fortunately, there were enough seasoned men in our outfit so that no tank crew was composed entirely of new arrivals.

I had the fortune—good or otherwise—to be under the company command of Captain Harkin. It seemed obvious to me that he knew his way around in this war thing and was probably a good commanding officer, but I nevertheless did my best to avoid him or at least keep out of his sight. He had liberated me from all my foolish fantasies of heroism, and that liberation settled me down to the moment-by-moment concerns of surviving. I no longer had a desire to stand out; I just wanted to fit in.

The workhorse of the American armored forces was the M4 Sherman Medium Tank, the chassis of which could be modified for many purposes. It was normally operated by a five-man crew. The tank to which I was assigned was a newer model, the M4A3, which had four guns: a 76-mm cannon, two .30-caliber machine guns, and one .50-caliber machine gun. Fully loaded, the tank weighed nearly thirty-five tons, was driven by a 450-horsepower Ford V-8 engine, and had a cruising speed of approximately twenty miles per hour.

My tank commander, Sergeant Joe Matira, was one of the lucky ones who had survived the Bulge and Aachen and Cologne, and he had a canny grasp of our local situation every moment. He was easy to know and easy to like. He made me feel like a significant member of the team. His designated location in the tank was a seat in the turret directly above and behind the gunner. He was in charge of receiving radio communications and carrying out orders from Company Command and of coordinating the actions of his crew. He had a tank weapon at his disposal, a .50-caliber machine gun attached to the top of the turret beside the turret hatch. It could be moved in all directions, including upward for antiaircraft protection.

Our loader—the guy in charge of loading the shells into the tank's cannon—was a portly T5 by the name of John Smith, to whom we immediately assigned the quite original nickname "Smitty." Smitty was a friendly guy, and he and I quickly became buddies.

Our driver, however, was someone I could count on to find terror in even the most unterrible situations. It was my fate to be linked to Graver, perhaps to the end of the earth. As a tank driver he was capable; as a combat soldier he had a few blank pages in his glossary. Graver was a decent chap who professed to be a born-again Southern Baptist Christian, but who early on sought his "salvation" in whatever source of alcohol he could find. He had to be numbed to be effective, yet he was seldom effective when he was numb—another incongruity of war. His driver's seat was in a hatch at the left front of the tank.

Our bow gunner–assistant driver was named Eddy Korstue, whom we automatically nicknamed "Corkscrew," an apt title it seemed, for this man was extremely odd. He was one of seven children, six of whom were girls and five of whom were older than he. He was the sort of fellow who could enjoy the company of females without thinking of how to maneuver one of them into bed—certainly not a real GI at heart! He was the tallest member of the crew—"six-four," he never tired of reminding us whenever an opportunity arose. But six-four is no asset in the cramped quarters of a Sherman tank. He was forever chewing bubblegum and popping bubbles. His lips had black patches around them from dried bubblegum. The bow gunner's position was in the right-front hatch of the tank, and his tank weapon was a ball-mounted .30-caliber machine gun that could be moved freely in all directions.

I was the gunner, and my job was to fire at anything to which I was directed by the tank commander, Sergeant Matira. My guns were the 76-mm tank cannon and a coaxially mounted .30-caliber machine gun, which meant that both cannon and machine gun moved together along the same axis. Both guns were zeroed in to hit the same target at 1,800 yards, which made it possible to use machine-gun tracers to target an object quickly and then fire the cannon to score. This was the sort of stuff I had learned at Fort Knox. But now I faced the brutal reality that it would make a real difference in whether or not I succeeded. No one was marking a scorecard, and I did not need an orientation lecture to inform me that this was no longer a dress rehearsal.

It was near the end of March, and the 3rd Armored Division—known as "Spearhead," since its function in the First Army was to serve as the point of the attack force—was bivouacked not far to the east of Bonn, in the Remagen bridgehead. The last major conflict the unit had engaged in (besides Bonn itself) had been the brutal battle to capture the city of Cologne on the "Sacred River," the Rhine. Cologne had been known as the "Queen City of the Rhine," but the queen had been deposed and decapitated, and the Allied forces had crossed the Sacred River. What lay ahead now was the final effort to drive the German forces to total capitulation.

Coincidence brought me into contact with a high school acquaintance of mine, Rudy Collins, a kid I never had much to do with in high school but whom I now found myself seeking out whenever I had the chance. Rudy had orange-red hair, freckles, was not much taller than I, and had a very cute blond sister named Ruthie, on whom I had once had a crush.

"She's got a boyfriend now, a gob. She's crazy about sailors' uniforms," Rudy sneered.

I tossed my head nonchalantly to hide my disappointment. "Too bad. She was sort of my type." The truth was, I knew that I wasn't Ruthie's type—at least not in high school. She was never available when I asked her to a school dance, and I had a personal principle that if a girl refused three dates in a row she was telling me something and I wouldn't ask her out again.

Rudy was a loader in one of the crews in my company, so I got to see him pretty often, especially during the few days we were bivouacked. I wondered why we had never had much to do with each other in high school, but the truth came out eventually that Rudy had thought I was a loser, simply because I was in trouble much of the time, flunked eleventh grade, and behaved pretty much as the class ass. I, on the other hand, had always thought that people (like Rudy) who worked hard and got good grades were jerks. But here, none of that mattered.

While we were exchanging adolescent trivia and thinking about the important things in life, such as girls, french fries, and hot dogs, the darker powers above us were arranging to put our lives in jeopardy. The valley of the Ruhr River was a major industrial target that, although heavily defended, demanded to be captured. Without its heavy industry, Germany could not hope to continue the war. However, to effect this capture would not be easy. The plan was to encircle the region as swiftly as possible and cut it off from its major defenses, one of which was the city of Paderborn, called the "Fort Knox of Germany," where panzer training was virtually a cottage industry, and where the Waffen-SS had a major training center.

On March 24, 1945, the orders came for the breakout from the Remagen bridgehead and the beginning of the final big push to drive across Germany and finish the war. Three great American armies, along with the forces of British field marshal Montgomery, began a major offensive. The First, Third, and Ninth U.S. Armies were across the Rhine and were joining in the Allies' *final solution* to the *Nazi problem*. Nothing short of unconditional and total surrender was ever considered as an option.

At 0400 hours on the morning of the twenty-fifth, the 32nd

and 33rd Armored Regiments took the lead of the division drive. Right behind us was the 703rd Tank Destroyer Battalion brandishing their long 90-mm cannons; and ready to move into physical action were the "Blitz Doughs" of the 36th Armored Infantry. These were followed by the 23rd Combat Engineers, the 83rd Light Reconnaissance, the mobile artillery, signalmen, medics, ordnance/maintenance, and supply units, known as the "Trains." I had never experienced anything like it in my life or in my most fantastic imaginings. Yet, whatever thrill I may have felt, I was soon to discover the unnerving sense of how unforgiving and relentless combat is.

I glanced over at Smitty, who was bouncing up and down and back and forth, appearing a bit ridiculous under his steel helmet. It occurred to me, when I looked back at a later time, that it was odd that we had never been issued tankers' helmets of the sort we always saw in the movies. Nor had I any other sidearm than my grease gun, which I kept on the tank deck outside rather than attempting to wrestle with it when getting in and out of the tank. Smitty gave me a confident smile as I sat down, which relaxed me a little. I smiled back and felt even more reassured by my own response. In truth, I was less afraid of the combat than I was of not measuring up.

Four columns of armor were moving on a wide front, passing through the positions of the grimy-faced, battle-weary doughboys of the 1st and 104th Infantry Divisions who had opened the way for this move. From my turret seat I could see very little of this. My only points of observation were through the limited window of my periscope and the small telescopic sight mounted in front of me on the turret. The "eyes" of the tank was the tank commander, whose head and shoulders usually poked out of the turret hatch. Joe had a pair of field glasses up to his eyes, scanning the terrain. Instead of a helmet, he was adorned with a radio headset, wires dangling into the hatch, where they were connected to the radio-intercom.

We had been on the move for only a short while when we encountered sudden fire from both flanks. The sounds of war—so much a part of the lives of men like Joe, who had been through so much—were less frightening to me than they were exhilarating. At Fort Knox we had been exposed to all sorts of quasi-combat sights, sounds, and actual physical sensations. I had romanticized it all then and found that I still did.

"Get ready!" Joe shouted into his intercom mike.

"Gunner ready!" I shouted back, as per training.

"Loader ready!" called Smitty, echoing my lead.

All around us the sound of shell fire and small arms in the vicinity told the story. The division had almost immediately run into severe resistance, and Joe picked up on the radio that Company B had already lost three tanks to land mines, probably Riegel mines. I couldn't see Graver, but I could imagine the condition of his underwear. Joe ordered him to stop and hold our position, giving him an opportunity to do his well-practiced turtle maneuver.

"Gunner!" Joe shouted. "Armored! On the right! About six hundred yards. Fire!"

"AP!" I shouted to Smitty and heard the clank of the breech closing as I found the armored car in my sight and fixed it in the crosshairs. "AP" stood for armor-piercing ammunition.

"On the way!" I called out as I tramped on the firing solenoid on the turret floor. I saw the tracer strike the ground not far behind the target vehicle and smelled the ammonia of the expended shell.

"Okay, kid," Joe shouted encouragingly. My right hand was trembling as I gripped the handle of the power traverse, which rotated the turret and controlled the gun's elevation.

"Down one hundred—fire!"

I dropped the elevation and fired again. In the scope I could see the tracer drive right into the side of the German armored car—my first score in actual combat! I shouted to Smitty.

"Loader—HE, quick!"

The "HE" stood for high-explosive, and I sent the round off immediately. As I had hoped, the shell followed its predecessor through the hole into the interior of the armored car, producing a gratifying flash for all to see.

But this was not a moment for congratulations. A tremendous metallic clank set my ears ringing. An enemy round had apparently glanced off our turret, nearly decapitating Joe.

"Outta here, driver, move out fast! They have our range!"

Graver, who had his hatch open enough to see, put the tank into gear and pulled sharply to the left, as he moved the tank ahead. This did the job. Ten yards behind us a German shell blew out a trench large enough to bury a tank.

"Good work, Graver!" came Joe's voice over the intercom. "Now get over to the right and stop behind that rise about fifty yards ahead."

All around us a whole war was going on, but the only war we knew at the moment was that of our tank against the German fire. The tank commander naturally has the advantage of being able to get the larger picture, and he has to be forever alert to every danger to his tank and to every opportunity to inflict damage on the enemy.

I discovered for myself during those first hours of combat what I had heard from others, that the hours don't exist—time stands still. Again and again we were bombarded with mortar fire and small arms, which are not much threat to armor, but I knew the doughs outside our tank were having a hell of a time. I had no way to judge how many shells I had fired or how many rounds of machine-gun ammo I had expended. Joe used the .50-caliber machine gun, which was mounted awkwardly on the turret by his hatch, very effectively when he had the chance, which was not very often. He had to climb out of the turret, exposing himself, to operate it.

Our division managed to gain about twelve miles that first day, fighting constantly. Move ahead—stop—fire—move again. At times it was possible to fire on the move, for our cannon had a gyro-stabilizer that compensated for the up-and-down motion of the tank to a large degree. It never occurred to me during that time that I hadn't eaten a bite, swallowed a drop of water, or relieved myself. I never even thought about it, though when we finally stopped, I noticed that I was not the only one whose pants were soaked in front, a condition I soon learned to control. In the semidarkness of early evening, much of the firing had stopped. Yet there was never any such thing as cessation of hostilities, even though darkness was wrapping itself around us. Artillery fire, intense at times, flashed almost continuously, rumbling like the thunder of a summer storm and cracking sharply in the air above as shells crisscrossed in the sky. I quickly learned to recognize the difference between the hollow ringing of the outgoing shells of our 155-mm "Long Toms" and the sharper ripping sound of incoming German 88s.

I reached up and tugged on Joe's trouser leg.

"Joe! Can we smoke?"

"Why not, kid? We're not hidin' from anybody. But not inside. You can give me one, too, if ya want."

Smitty had located a box of K rations and was chewing on a dried fruit bar.

"Y'know, I hate these things," he grumbled and kept on stuffing it into his face and chewing.

Joe and I climbed out onto the deck and lit up. Smitty followed suit.

"Are we here for the night or what?" I asked Joe, who cupped his cigarette in his hand.

"Damned if I know. I can only guess. We could move out at daylight or even before that." He saw the fatigue in my face. "Look, kid, we don't have a bedtime here. Try to get some sleep for now."

I barely heard that last word before I was down on the gunner's seat asleep—sitting up. The thunder of shells exploding faded into an undefined hum.

Joe nodded to Smitty. "You catch a couple, too. Looks like the boys in the bows are already ahead of ya."

He draped himself over the turret, his radio crackling in his ears, and dozed.

It was not as though there had been a time-out, as in a football game. I had to get used to the idea that there really were no rules to follow, no daily regimen of personal activities such as eating, drinking, hygiene, recreation, or sleeping. This was not regimental training anymore. Yet despite the inhumanity of the incessant violence going on everywhere at once, life quickly became a routine of noise, dirt, fatigue, anxiety, and the constant struggle to keep going. But for the fever of the combat itself and one's own little bit part in the undramatic and confused action, life would have devolved into a mindless, zombielike existence.

Before sunrise on March 26, our unit, Task Force Welborn, part of Combat Command B under General Truman Boudinot, moved eastward toward the city of Altenkirchen, where the Fifteenth German Army had its headquarters. Altenkirchen was known to have heavy defenses, both in the city itself and on the forested heights to the north. Even before we got to the city, we came up against stubborn resistance, especially from artillery and tanks. Our company followed A Company. B Company was at the point of the column and was taking losses from direct artillery fire, particularly from the 88s. Both A Company and I Company moved ahead and joined the action. We succeeded in breaking through these preliminary defenses, but as we approached Altenkirchen, the intensity of German resistance increased enormously.

I was vaguely aware inside the tank of strikes against the German forces by fighter-bombers, which destroyed many enemy tanks and artillery emplacements. I came to realize what was meant by "softening up" the enemy. Nevertheless, we had no easy time of it. Our forward movement was fairly constant throughout the morning, and for a while our company seemed to be getting off easy. But as the afternoon came on, we made direct contact with German panzers. It was the first time I had been up against them, and I soon learned for myself the bitter truth that the firepower of the Sherman tank, even with the

76-mm cannon, left much to be desired. Despite that discovery, I had my first success in knocking out an enemy tank that afternoon. It was an encouraging feeling and gave me renewed confidence in our equipment.

But I saw Smitty die that second day of combat, and I felt numb. For the first time in my life I became a believer in a personal death. As awful as the experience was, I had reason to be grateful for that revelation. I would owe my own survival to it. It shouldn't have happened, of course. No one is *supposed* to die—at least not *that* young, or in *that* way. But Smitty was dead, and somehow I felt as though I was to blame. We had been outside on the tank deck, filling our canteens from a water can, during an extremely brief lull in the action, and I had climbed back into the turret before he did. Joe was crouching behind the tank, grabbing a quick smoke. I had just returned to my gunner's seat when Joe stuck his head in the hatch and yelled, "Smitty's been hit!"

I climbed back out and saw my friend lying on the tank deck with part of his face missing. I couldn't believe he was dead, so I got very close and I saw one eye open slightly.

"He's alive!" I shouted to Joe. "Get a medic!"

I saw a slight sideward movement of his head and knew he had died—even as I watched.

My first impulse was to touch the body, but I recoiled when I heard Joe's voice beside me.

"C'mon, kid, leave 'im right there and get inside or we'll all be dead!"

Corkscrew had to fill in as loader, and it was not the same. He didn't belong in a tank—too damn big—but he did okay lifting shells out of the rack in the turret floor and slamming them into the breech. Still, it didn't help that he had to keep his steel helmet on to protect his head, which kept banging against the turret top. In the intensity of the action that followed, I completely forgot about who was doing what. For the moment I forgot how immediate death could be and how vulnerable we all were. I focused only on the range marks in my telescopic sight, the machine-gun trigger on the power traverse handle I was gripping, and the targets I was searching for. The turret smelled like wet diapers, and time once more stopped.

Our forces had outflanked the Germans at Altenkirchen, and they literally fled to the hills just north of the city. CCB spent the night just west of the city. It was necessary to take turns standing guard, each crew taking care of its own tank. Fatigue in combat is not like being tired after a day's work. It penetrates every sinew and every nerve, and a good night's sleep seldom comes your way, and rarely cures it.

The style of combat in this war differed radically from that of its predecessor of 1914–18, where movement was stalled, where men suffered unbelievable misery and indescribable agonies in muddy, rat-filled trenches and considered a two-mile advance, won at enormous human cost, a major accomplishment—yet as often as not forfeited it soon after in retreat. Stagnation was for them a way of life.

But technology had converted those disease-ridden trenches into mobile tracked vehicles that could serve as mini-fortresses one moment and pursue the enemy the next. Armor on tracks and wheels—half-tracks, armored cars, tanks, and tank destroyers—gave this war a new kind of action. The new dimension in this war also included combat from the air, something our ancestor war was not ready to take seriously, but something without which we could not have succeeded.

At this point in the war, following the crossing of the Rhine, our object was to take ground and pursue the slowly retreating Germans. They were a desperate and very determined enemy who were forbidden to consider retreat as anything other than a tactical maneuver for an advantage, for whom defeat was not a legitimate concept, and who had been inoculated with the idea that death was preferable to surrender.

Our tank was not actually hit that day, though a lot of shrapnel from mortar fire had found some of our guys—including Smitty. "Our guys" meant our armored infantry doughs who fought along with the tanks. Our duffel bags, which contained our worldly possessions and were fastened on the deck wherever we could find a suitable place, were riddled with rips and tears. My own bag had two large holes in it, and I imagined that one day I would reach in to get some underwear and grab the jagged edge of a piece of shrapnel.

After two days of combat, I had become a veteran tanker. I knew that Joe respected me as a gunner. For once in my adolescent life, I didn't feel like a foolish class ass, a refreshing experience for me. I no longer had any desire to be the center of attention or to be popular. Indeed, the war was conditioning me to be the opposite.

On the twenty-seventh of March, we had a momentary lull. Joe told me that he had been requested by Captain Harkin to compose a letter to Smitty's parents. The captain was charged with expressing condolences when time allowed, but he wasn't "good with words." He had hoped that Joe could do it.

"I'm no good at writing," Joe grumbled. "I'd give a cigar to the guy who could do it instead of me."

I might have been a jackass in high school, but I knew how to write.

"I'll write it," I offered.

"You?" Joe was incredulous. "You can write?"

"Yeah."

"Okay, do it!"

And I did.

Dear Mr. and Mrs. Smith,

    We know you have heard of John's untimely death in the service of his country. Every man of his crew and every man in the entire division wants you to know that our war effort will suffer from his loss. He was a gallant soldier and a friend to all who knew him. He never did anything wrong and always did everything right. Please accept our condolences and our hopes that his death will not have been in vain. We will all miss him.

                                            Sincerely,

Joe commented that maybe "entire division" and "our war effort will suffer from his loss" were kind of overdone, even for bereaved parents.

"After all, the kid just joined the outfit."

He was right, of course, so I modified the letter to make it more believable, more personal, as though I was writing it for myself. Apparently Captain Harkin approved of the final result, because he made a point of stopping by our tank to thank me.

"Nice letter, Corporal. I appreciate it." He paused, then added,

"I get the idea that you're a hell of a better gunner than you are a war hero." He grinned, and as he left I was certain I saw his shoulders vibrating up and down. He was actually laughing, something I didn't know he could do.

The captain's compliment did not make up for the loss of a buddy, but it was something I could hang on to. I had actually known Smitty for only a few days. This was a strange world where time was stretched, twisted, bent back upon itself, of critical significance one moment and virtually without meaning the next. Strangely, after another day or so my memory of him got repressed. But I hung on to the captain's compliment. Smitty was dead, but I still had a war to live.

Another peculiarity of the war presented itself that day. Four German deserters wandered into our area looking for something to eat and hoping to be captured. I was amazed. What kind of a war was this where soldiers begged to be captured and their enemy chased them away? At every group of GIs they came to they would place their hands upon their heads and shout "Kamerad!" And each time they would be run off with something like "Raus, you bastards, or we'll shoot your asses worse than we have already." I felt sorry for them, but I'd had enough trouble with "capturing prisoners" for one war. I ducked behind the tank so they wouldn't see me, because I knew I couldn't treat them that way. I hadn't been around this war long enough for that. It was gratifying, though, to see a couple of crew members from one of the companies share rations with them. But no one took them prisoner.

By March 28th, after all-night combat by most of our elements, the division reached Marburg, a center of staunch, rigid Nazism. The main story here was prisoners and more prisoners.

So many German prisoners were taken that there was much confusion about accommodating them. Along with men, the Germans had lost an unacceptably large amount of equipment. I stood on the tank deck and watched the flow of prisoners moving along like a river, and wondered how much more the Germans had to give.

At Marburg, the 3rd Armored Division got its orders to attack north to Paderborn. Unknown to us mere combat soldiers, March 29th was to be for us a history-making day in the Second World War. Not that it was an occasion of the war's most memorable battle or the greatest destruction of German matériel and men. It was the longest single drive made in one day by Allied forces in Germany in the entire war. We covered more than ninety miles (144 kilometers) that day, from Marburg to within thirty miles of Paderborn, from the southern part of the Ruhr valley to its northern perimeter, making the encirclement of the Ruhr valley a virtual certainty. The fact that a number of towns were taken along the way made our speed all the more remarkable. The secret of the operation's success was precisely this speed, which truly surprised the enemy. No one could have predicted a drive like that. And even when the German forces at Paderborn got wind of what was happening, there was disbelief among their elite command.

At Paderborn, elements of the SS Panzer Replacement and Training Center and the SS Reconnaissance Training Regiment moved into positions of defense from which they were ready to "blitz" the invaders. Here was the last obstacle to the full cutoff of the Ruhr.

It was warm for March, and the concrete highway we were traveling was cluttered with rubber from tank treads. Most of our tanks had tracks with rubber blocks instead of all steel, and the heat build-up and constant pounding of the treads caused pieces of rubber to break off.

Graver was okay for about two-thirds of the day, but Corkscrew took over the driving during the afternoon. Steering a tank is done by pulling on brake handles, left or right, while gunning the engine, and Graver was getting cramps in his left arm. We stopped along the way only to refuel. When nature made its requirements known, whatever spectators there might have been were treated to the ridiculous spectacle of men urinating from their tanks or "dumping" into their steel helmets (one of the most versatile army implements, incidentally, in World War II) and tossing it away as they traveled, rarely without unwelcome consequences. The seat I was attached to had reduced my buns to a couple of large bruises. I took to kneeling on the floor of the turret, just to relieve the pressure. It was a grueling day and one I would not forget. Like everyone else, I was glad when I heard the command to halt. But our relief was short-lived. The enemy at Paderborn by now knew that we were coming, and they were preparing a reception for us.

CHAPTER 3

CLOSING

THE ROSE POCKET

It was an incredible world I had found myself in, a world that allowed no time for acclimation and seldom forgave mistakes. Nothing could surprise me at this point, so when Smitty's replacement as loader climbed aboard even as we traveled those monotonous ninety miles from Marburg, I saw nothing odd about it.

"Name's Pete, Pete Kowanski," he shouted in a high-pitched voice above the racket of the idling tank engine.

Kowanski was a very big guy, not as tall as Corkscrew but twice as heavy. His size came not so much from fat as from his big frame. His hands were huge and when he took off his helmet I saw that his short blond hair was getting thin.

"Irwin," I shouted back. "Jack Irwin."

This new man was obviously not new to the war. I judged him to be about twenty-five years old, very old in my book, and I soon learned that he was a sergeant, that both he and Joe had been to-gether in the 3rd Armored since D-day plus two, and that Joe had requested that Kowanski be assigned to our crew. There was a reassuring air about Kowanski, a quiet confidence and a savvy manner. Joe and I had been riding on the deck of the tank, along with seven armored infantry doughs, when he climbed up onto our tank out of the peep that had brought him.

"This is your gunner!" Joe shouted to Kowanski. "Don't let his pint size fool you. He's a damned good gunner!"

Kowanski nodded his head. "Good! Just lost a good gunner in Company B."

It turned out that Kowanski had been tank commander in one of the Company B tanks that had been knocked out several days ago. He had lost his gunner and driver, and no replacement tank was forthcoming at present.

He stuck out his hand to the group of doughs riding on the deck and hollered, "Glad to see you guys here! I was afraid you'd all been killed."

The armored infantry boys all grinned as they reached out their hands. It was as though they were part of our own crew, since we had to work closely with them. Kowanski knew all of them. They had been on the battle beat since Belgium—two of them since France.

Pete nodded toward me. "What d'ya think of the kid here?"

"He's no more of a kid than Ah am," said one dough, taking off his helmet. "Ah'm just barely seventeen. Lied 'bout my age to get in."

He didn't look it—tall, a very coarse beard, browned face, rugged features, hair graying at the sides. I'd have pegged him for about thirty, maybe more.

"Bullshit!" laughed Kowanski.

I got to know the names of the doughs—"Ugly," "Mildew," "Scrunch," "Mad Dog," "Pisser," "Shithead," and "Lobes." I knew they had real names embossed on their dog tags, but these were their combat names. What stuck out most about these guys was the fact that every one of them came from somewhere in Dixie. Not merely the South, but the *hills* of the South, the *rural* South. I felt at home, Yankee though I was. It had seemed to me that half of Fort Knox had come from the backcountry somewhere south of the Mason-Dixon Line. And invariably one of them had a banjo, someone else a guitar, another a harmonica, and always there was a fiddle.

Something I enjoyed about those Rebs besides their music was their quick wit and funny expressions. They had a way of saying things that cut to the meat and made me laugh at the same time. I had had a first sergeant in basic training who spoke unsmilingly of the colonel who was to inspect us: "Ah wouldn't say he was chickenshit, but he sure as hell has henhouse ways."

I was beginning to get a grasp on this new world, with its sense of universal camaraderie in opposition to a common enemy. Men of different organizations, as yet unknown to me, would be my comrades automatically should I meet them. It mattered not that in ordinary civilian life I might not give them so much as a glance. In this environment we were aware of a common bond between us and were ready to ignore the potential contempt we might have had for one another under different circumstances. One could not really call it friendship, though friendships were born every day in combat. But while comradeship is brother to friendship, they are not really the same thing.

Sometime late in the afternoon, a peep carrying two men

came alongside of our tank. The one on the passenger side was obviously an officer. He had a crew cut, stiff graying hair, a serious, handsome face, and a big frame. He looked up at us and touched a forefinger to his brow in a salute and said, "My helmet's off to you men—keep it up!"

"Know who that was?" Kowanski asked as the peep moved ahead, stopping briefly alongside each tank.

"No," I shouted, as the engine roared. "Who is he?"

Kowanski grinned slightly. "Just the best fucking officer in the whole goddamn U.S. Army. That was General Rose, division commander."

I knew the name, but it had not made an impression on me before this moment.

"This isn't the first time I've seen him," said Kowanski. "Spent several hours with him, pinned down in a ditch along a road in Belgium. He's a GI, just like the rest of us. Always up front with his men."

I didn't quite realize what that fingertip meant to guys like Joe and Pete and the doughs, but I knew I was included, and I gained a deeper sense of the division's esprit de corps.

It was dark when we finally stopped. It had been a long, grueling day and I didn't have the slightest idea where we were, not that it would have meant anything to me if I had. I had no grasp at all of the geography involved.

"We're south of Paderborn," Kowanski offered. "Nieder Marsberg—I saw a sign."

That information really didn't tell me much. I was tired, even though I'd had little to do except ride the tank. The one thing, however, that really stuck with me was the sight of the crowds of refugees we saw that day, walking and stumbling along the road leading away from the city—old people, small children, mothers with babies slung across their fronts, carrying whatever they could, some pushing wobbly baby carriages or pulling little wagons loaded with their belongings. It was a sight I would see too often, refugees leaving their homes to escape the expected invasion and destruction of their cities. For a brief moment, I thought of home and my mother. She had had a heart attack not long before I left for the army and was only slightly improved when I visited during a delay on my way to Fort Dix before going to Camp Shanks, in New York, and thence on board the *Queen Mary* for Europe. That seemed like half a lifetime ago.

We had arrived at Nieder Marsberg around 2200 hours. Graver and Corkscrew went off somewhere in the darkness and returned about twenty minutes later with four or five bottles of homemade wine, requisitioned from the cellar of some frightened Germans. I soon learned that this is how wars are really fought. The shooting and blowing up of houses is but a cover for young bucks to have a time of it—whenever they can. "In the army," a cadreman at Fort Knox once told me, "you do just what you can get away with." Here it was not so much a matter of "getting away with it" as it was of finding the opportunity. They both got drunk. To the best of my knowledge, Graver rarely sobered up again during the war.

I thought about Graver and the other men of the outfit. We were an assortment of men and adolescents, brought together in a common struggle to survive and prevail. We all had much to learn, both the older veterans and the newer replacements. For some it was more difficult than for others. I realized that I had a long way to go to become a man. I was having a serious conflict within myself. Here I was, an eighteen-year-old virgin in an army full of guys, many of whom believed you weren't a man till you "had a dose" (of clap, that is, gonorrhea). Seemed like an awful price to pay for manhood. How many virgin boys surrendered their chastity and good health to the cause of manhood during this conflict is a matter of pure speculation. Even more interesting is the question of how many boasted that they did, but didn't. There were many good reasons why they should not, and these were not particularly moral or religious reasons.

Sleep more or less just happened rather than being something anyone actually did. Despite the commotion around me, I slept until some ungodly hour before the sun rose, when I felt Joe's boot on my shoulder as I lay on the tank deck.

"C'mon, kid. Get your ass in gear! We got a hell of a day ahead. We got SS waitin' for us, ready to shoot our fuckin' balls off!"

I was instantly awake.

Pete was checking out the ammo in the floor of the turret as I climbed into my gunner's seat. He looked over at me and said seriously, "Y'know, kid, if you're even half as good as Matira thinks you are, I'll be satisfied." I smiled gratefully. His opinion meant a lot to me. I wanted to be a respected member of the crew, someone who—

"Graver! Get this iron coffin revved up!"

Reality again!

Graver was in a stupor and didn't respond.

"Goddamn it, man, this is a hell of a time to be drunk! You'd better get that engine going or I'll carry out my own court martial with this forty-five!"

Somehow, that worked. The tank engine roared, and Graver managed a slurred question: "Where to?"

Joe restrained himself. "We're playing follow-the-leader. The tank in front of you is your leader—just don't crash into it. Ya hear me? You drunken son of a bitch!"

Then it was instant combat. We had gone only a short distance when we came under fire. Panzerfausts! These hand-held German bazookas were fired broadside at close range against tanks, sometimes causing molten metal to spray the inside. They used recoilless, disposable launchers, and any kid could fire one—and often did. They came with a variety of warheads and served a wide range of destructive ends.

"Graver! Get around that house over there—on your right!"

Pete pushed the barrel of a carbine through the turret basket and jabbed Graver's right shoulder.

"Right! Right!"

Graver did what he was ordered to do, but when he saw the flash of cannon fire immediately in front of him, he pulled back the brake handles, shifted, and backed up—directly into the house. In fact, he did such an excellent job of it that the turret was jammed into the house and couldn't be moved.

"Goddamn it to hell!" Joe shouted. "Get yer asses out of the tank! Bail out! Bail out!!"

Joe had a point. A tank with a turret that could not traverse and get on target was absolutely useless. It had no firepower and was a sitting duck.

Joe was out and I managed to climb out despite the wall of the house partly blocking the hatch. Pete was right behind me but had a harder time of it. But Graver and Corkscrew didn't show. Pete climbed over the front of the tank and pulled Graver out of the driver's hatch and dropped him in the dirt. He couldn't find

Corkscrew, who was out of sight in an alcoholic stupor on the floor of the hatch, so he came back and ran to join us behind the building.

"Those bastards deserve what they get!" he grumbled.

We waited and watched what was happening.

"You got a weapon, kid?" Pete asked me.

"Uh, no. I just got out—"

"Take this," he murmured, as he handed me the carbine he had brought from the turret. Like Joe, he had a .45 in his hand.

The three of us were crouched around the corner of the house, just watching. The Germans appeared to be backing off, but we could never be sure what they were up to. They might well have a second wave waiting for us to begin pursuit only to fall into a trap.

"I can't stand this!" Pete grumbled after several minutes and dashed around the corner. A moment later, I heard the roar of the tank engine and felt the house shake. Pete soon managed to break the tank free from its prison, something only a sober man could have done.

"C'mon," yelled Joe, who ran to the tank and climbed into the driver's seat. I got into the turret, where Pete was already loading a shell in the breech.

"Let's make these count," he shouted. "You pick the targets!"

And I did. The barrel of the cannon eventually got so hot that now and then a round would fire off before I had a chance to trigger it. Joe kept maneuvering the tank to make us a poor target and to give me shots. Those were mostly dug-in infantry and light armor. I ran out of .30-caliber, and without a bow gunner our firepower was diminished. But our HE shells wrought some real havoc with the German infantry behind the stone walls and in buildings in front of us.

Our company got spread out, and for a while we had no visual contact with other crews. That's a disconcerting feeling, especially with our diminished crew and firepower. Yet we seemed to have fortune on our side. At one point, I shot almost randomly at a low wall in front of us, and to my amazement an entire bazooka squad came out from behind another section of the wall, their hands on their heads. When I first saw them I wondered whether they could survive the intense gunfire all around them. In fact, one of them was hit and the others raced back behind the wall. I knew they no longer had their weapons, so I didn't shoot at that point of the wall.

And then the shooting subsided. The enemy were backing off, seeking a retreat that would leave them a sufficient reserve to engage us again. At least fifty bodies, mostly German, were scattered around the area, and the homes of yesterday were the rubble of today. The stucco houses were pockmarked from bullets or had gaping holes from shells and bazookas. Some were in ruins. We could see the evidence of the hasty German retreat in the form of abandoned vehicles and weapons littering the entire area. The smoldering hulk of a King Tiger tank blocked the road in front of us, so that there was no way around it without damaging the house next to it. Joe did what had to be done so we could move on.

Incredibly, people came out of their houses and were everywhere wandering around the debris, some crying, some just gazing in bewilderment. The doughs were trying to get them to go back inside, and some really strange sights presented themselves. We saw a small woman turn on a big GI and start pummeling him with both fists when he tried to make her go into a house.

"My money's on the old woman," grinned Joe.

Graver came dragging himself over to the tank. He was not feeling good, to say the least. Corkscrew had been slumped in the bow gunner's hatch the whole time. He looked pretty awful. But we had no pity to spare for either of them, and Joe was threatening to have them both shot if they pulled another stunt like that. He really meant it. Graver complained that he felt as though he already had been shot.

"You could have holes all over you," yelled Joe, "and not even know it in your condition. You guys deserted us in combat, do you realize that? What do you know about the Articles of War?"

It seemed obvious to me that both men realized the gravity of their action, and I doubted that they would be that stupid again. But stupidity, it seems, often knows no bounds.

Though I was only vaguely aware of the larger picture, our regiment and the 32nd Armored Regiment, both part of Task Force Welborn, had been pressing northward in hopes of joining with forces heading eastward across the northern perimeter of the Ruhr valley. Lippstadt, a city about twenty miles west of Paderborn, was to be the point of contact between Task Force Kane from the 3rd Armored, which was heading west from Et-teln, and the tanks of the 2nd Armored "Hell on Wheels" Division, which was moving eastward and thereby cutting off the whole Ruhr industrial region. The plan worked magnificently and certainly shortened the war, but not without a high price in lives and equipment. The 2nd Armored Division had met with savage resistance and had lost many tanks, weapons, and men in the drive. The 2nd and 3rd Armored Divisions were the only heavy armored divisions in the U.S. Army, and both were coordinated in this final push across Germany.

It was the thirtieth of March, and the division was concentrated in an area north of the city of Etteln, confronting dug-in infantry and tanks and receiving a great deal of fire. Our tank was low on ammo, especially .30-cal. machine-gun belts. Corkscrew had to split what he had with me. Pete warned me to go easy on the HE—only a few shells left. I strained to see what was going on through my periscope, when a tremendous explosion shook our tank. The tank in front of us in the column took a hit from a German self-propelled gun, effectively blocking our passage and that of the tanks behind us. We were all standing targets.

Joe yelled, "Bail out! Fast!"

As luck had it, our deserted tank was then hit by the same self-propelled gun and appeared to be disabled.

"Shit!" exclaimed Joe, slamming his helmet onto the ground.

He waited until things looked safe and crawled over to the tank, gave it a quick examination, and hurried back.

"Could be worse," he growled. "Soon as they get things cleared up, we're gonna put that son of a bitch back into action."

I wondered about the turret. Would it turn? Could I fire the gun?

"Don't know," he answered quietly. "Have to take a chance."

Once the way was cleared around the disabled tank in front of us, we remounted and discovered that there had been more noise than damage. I found that the turret still worked. We guessed that a high-explosive round had struck the front armor plate and glanced off, causing minimal damage.

That afternoon, as we were moving slowly, I spotted a boy no more than twelve years of age running toward us with a Panzerfaust grasped in his hands. He was wearing the uniform of the Hitler Youth.

"Joe!" I shouted. "That kid!"

"Kill 'im!" Joe screamed.

And I did. A short burst from the .30-cal. machine gun and he was on the ground, limp and quite dead on top of his Panzerfaust. And I felt no emotion at that moment except relief.

"Good work, kid," Joe shouted, and I accepted his praise.

Death is the very essence of war, but not all deaths are equal. A twelve-year-old boy counts for little, but the loss of a great general calls for great lamentation. Such was the case when the division got word that its beloved commander, Major General Maurice Rose, had been killed. His party had consisted of only three peeps, two motorcycles, and an armored car. How it all happened remains obscure, but according to one report a German panzer blocked the road and the party tried to force their way past. When it turned out there was insufficient room, they were stopped. General Rose and his driver placed their hands on their heads, but for some reason the tank commander fired his "burp gun" at the group, killing General Rose. It may be that when the general lowered his hands to remove his pistol belt, the German tank commander feared that he was going for his gun. No one really knows, but General Rose had been killed, and the division had lost its commander.

So popular was the general with the men of the division that many took his death quite personally, especially the older combat veterans like Joe Matira and Pete Kowanski. They didn't say much, but it was obvious from their somber curses and sullen demeanor that they were crushed—and vengeful. I was reaching a deeper understanding by the hour of the close relationships that develop in combat, relationships not based on rank or the specifics of personal friendship. It was something deeper, something almost spiritual.

The killing of General Rose may have proven as much of a loss to the Germans as it was to us, for the anger and determination his death generated in his men reflected the spirit he instilled in the division by his courage and example. The men of the 3rd Armored Division had enormous respect for their commander and would not forget him as they fought to justify his steadfast confidence in them.

Paderborn was one of the few major defenses that the Germans had at this point. Here we were faced with desperate troops who still believed in the Third Reich and were ready to die for the Führer. We were briefed by Captain Harkin, who made it clear to us that *this* enemy was completely nuts and would commit any atrocity or make any sacrifice for the Führer. We also learned from him that the new commander of the division was Brigadier General Doyle O. Hickey, a battle-tested combat officer whose pipe was a permanent fixture in his mouth. I got the idea from Joe and Pete that we would be in good hands.

"I am required to say this," Captain Harkin continued. "We really don't want any more prisoners than necessary. Now listen good! I'm *not* telling you to shoot men who are surrendering. Everyone got that? Just because the Krauts have no consciences doesn't mean that we don't either. Any questions?"

None.

"Good! Now let's give 'em some payback!"

It was the first of April. We had restocked our ammunition racks and were up to par, ready to continue our relentless push, weary though we all were. Engines started roaring, and the tanks of I Company joined with those of B Company to lead the task force into Paderborn. At the time, I had no idea of the size and complexity of the operation we were involved in. Joe told us that he understood that there were to be three task forces moving on Paderborn from different directions. Task Force Welborn would be attacking from the east of the city.

The encirclement of the Ruhr region had been successful largely because of the speed with which it had been accomplished. It had been named the "Ruhr Pocket," but it was renamed "Rose Pocket" by the 3rd Armored Division to honor its fallen commander, and that became its official name in the First Army records. The German defense forces had been caught off guard and confused, and many thousands of enemy troops had already surrendered, to be herded into overcrowded containment pens pending more permanent arrangements. It was clear to us that *they*, at least, knew Germany's cause was hopeless.

Graver surprised me. He wasn't able to get anything to drink, yet he held his own in spite of that. He was a good driver—when he had control of himself. And Corkscrew made a deal with Pete to spell him as loader once in a while, just to get the kinks out of his own cramped legs. A group of AI doughs were riding on the deck, where they would be ready for action when the time came. Most of the armored infantry rode in half-tracks until we met resistance, but quite a few rode on the tanks. Scrunch and Squawky actually shot craps on the back deck of our tank, where wind and chill and noise made winning and losing a serious challenge.

By the gray light of the early cloudy morning we could see fire and smoke creating a weird, phantasmagoric scene above the city of Paderborn. The city had been, and was being, pounded by Allied fighter-bombers and shell fire and was suffering serious destruction. I stood with my head out of the turret hatch; Joe was standing on the back deck behind the turret.

"Wow!" was all I could manage.

Joe chewed on his cigar.

"Pretty damn impressive, don't ya think?" He watched. "They're beaten but they don't know it. That's a bad kind of enemy! Bunch of fucking fanatics."

And they were. I was amazed that despite the incessant bombardment and strafing, the German forces at Paderborn came out of the city on the attack. Tanks, tank destroyers, self-propelled guns—everything they could pull together. We moved off the road and across the muddy fields to engage them.

I heard Joe's voice on the intercom saying, "We're gonna flank 'em. They'll get it from the front and both sides. Keep 'er loaded, Pete! Kid, keep your face to that sight!"

The German armor formed a line of defense ahead of us and began showing enormous firepower. I could see some of what was going on, but not much. The ride was rough. Several times Graver got stuck in the gluey mud but was able to back us out and move on. All of the American tanks were firing at the Germans, and they in turn unleashed on us everything they could muster, which was tremendous. Joe picked the targets, and I tried to hit them. One contact was with a King Tiger, one of Germany's most feared tanks. I was not the only gunner firing at it, for I saw tracers coming from other directions as well. I don't know who made the hit, but that mighty Tiger growled its last as somebody's round damaged the turret. Its crew scrambled from the hatches and abandoned the smoking remains as GI machine-gun fire strafed them. All appeared to be casualties.

The morning grew lighter, but the sun never showed itself. The only measure I had as to how things were going was the intensity of the German fire coming against us. The armored infantry doughs—several hundred of them—had scattered between the tanks, moving with the armor and taking losses from mortar and machine-gun fire. Again and again I sprayed German infantry with my .30-caliber to protect our doughs. Corkscrew showed that he, too, could be a real menace to the Germans. The way he maneuvered his .30-cal. gun in every direction was a work of art.

As we slowly approached the city, the German armor retreated in orderly echelon formations and gradually took up new positions inside the city. In front of our group was an impressive array of Tigers. And I could see the muted flashes from their cannon fire. We had almost reached the tanks immediately in front of us when a shell glanced off of our right sponson.

Joe shouted, "Did you see it?"

Yes, I had seen it, the tank that had fired the shell, and I fired back even as Joe spoke. I saw the tracer of the round that scored a direct hit streak heavenward—not a good sign. I was coming to realize that my 76 was no match for that kind of armor. But I fired again, and this time the tracer seemed to have hit the tank, but I couldn't be sure. All I noticed was that it did not ricochet.

Then Pete yelled, "That's the last AP!"

"So give 'em HE!" yelled Joe through the intercom. "Give 'em *hell*!"

One thing about HE was its concussion, which could incapacitate turret mechanisms, tracks, and other moving parts, even if the shell failed to penetrate the armor. Tanks could be completely disabled this way.

As all of this was going on, I happened to catch a glimpse of one of our guys from another crew actually climbing out of his tank, pulling down his pants, dumping his load, and, without wiping, climbing back into the tank, pants still halfway off. Desperation is the mother of heroic expedience.

We worked our way into Paderborn, where the Germans had abandoned their earlier positions and established new defenses among the houses, leaving much of their armor behind. The infantrymen were engaged in hellish house-to-house combat, and we had the job of doing whatever we could to cover and assist them. I had the dubious honor of shooting some walls out so the doughs could get inside.

The battle for Paderborn seemed to go on forever. It was never clear to me at any moment whether we were succeeding in driving the Germans back or not. A score against a tank or an armored car or our firing against the omnipresent German infantry with their diabolic Panzerfausts never seemed sufficient to bring them to their knees. Yet eventually, after hours of fierce combat, the worst of the struggle was over, and none but the most stubborn pockets of suicidal SS troops held out.

Paderborn was, for all intents and purposes, taken. But it would be several days before the entire region was cleared. Many thousands of German prisoners were being herded into extremely crowded containment pens. Eventually they would be moved into regular prison camps. For them the war was over, even if they couldn't go home.

There is something about the semiconclusion of a battle-not-lost that encourages men to continue to believe in a future. If we can do this here, we can do it again there! The feeling lasts precisely until the next engagement.

CHAPTER 4

TOWNS AND RIVERS

It was pathetic to see Graver succumb once again to the opportunity to numb himself with some "vino," bartered from a couple of doughs who were out of cigarettes. (The term "vino" for wine or booze in general persisted among GIs after the Italian campaign.) We were certainly not on leave, though the intensity of the resistance had diminished for the time being. Maybe he thought that so long as he had his New Testament in his pocket he'd be somehow protected in his crapulence. I never actually saw him *read* it. Corkscrew and I knew that he managed to keep a bottle hidden in the driver's hatch, but we said nothing about it, and I wondered what Joe would do when he saw the condition of his driver.

The boys from supply had done a great job of getting ammo to all companies, even under fire. We now had our full complement of both AP and HE shells and .30-cal. and .50-cal. machine-gun belts. It's a worrisome feeling to be low on—or, worse, out of—ammunition of one kind or another.

This was a confusing time, as we tried to finish off the enemy in the city and the area around Paderborn. We could never be sure at any moment when some German armor would appear from between buildings to confront us. Worse than the tanks were the Germans' new tank destroyers (TDs), which carried a 128-mm cannon. We saw two of these low-profile moving pillboxes, the second of which selected us for its target. Its handicap, however, was that it had no turret and could move the cannon only a few degrees in either direction. Nevertheless, it did manage to get us in view and fired, missing us by about ten yards.

"Graver—move!" shouted Joe.

Graver's head wasn't altogether clear, but he managed to move us out of range of the German TD, giving me an opportunity to fire two rounds before it could get at us again.

"Move again!" shouted Joe.

Each time we moved, I managed to get off a couple of rounds before we were targeted once more. I was not having any more success than Jerry was. The one hit I scored simply ricocheted off the heavy armor. I realized finally that we would get nowhere so long as that monster was able to move.

"Pete!" I shouted. "HE!"

The breech clanged shut. I took my time aiming at his front drive sprocket. I shouted "Bingo!" as the drive sprocket shattered. The crew of the TD were bailing out, and I was unloading my co-ax .30-cal. all over them. How many were hit I couldn't tell. I heaved a sigh of relief. Pete gave me the "V" sign with his right hand, and I returned it with mine.

"I never saw one of those before," I hollered to Pete.

"They're Germany's latest TD," yelled Pete, who had his face pressed against the periscope. "We don't want to see too many of them!"

I shuddered when I thought of what that monster could do to us and prayed that we would not have to face any more.

It seemed strange to me that Joe hadn't got angry with Graver for hitting the bottle again, but apparently Joe and Graver had come to some kind of understanding. Later, Joe explained that he knew what Graver was going through. He'd seen it before. Some guys can't make it without assistance from alcohol. The deal was, however—no drunkenness.

"As long as he can hold up his end . . ." said Joe, his voice trailing off.

I realized that Graver was just as normal as any of us—we all pissed our pants and wanted to hide sometimes. It wasn't Graver who wasn't normal; it was the war that wasn't normal. It isn't normal to spend your time destroying cities and killing people and cheering when the other guys get killed. And I knew it wasn't normal for me to put Smitty out of my mind, or to feel no remorse for a kid I had shot to death point-blank. And the thought haunted me in my darker moments that I perhaps was a murderer. This was no football game, and we weren't playing. We didn't tackle anyone; we killed them.

On the following day, we encountered pockets of enemy resistance. At times, it seemed that the Germans were getting a second wind. But their devotion to their cause, while not half-hearted, was doomed by the great odds against them and their lack of men and matériel. As hard as it is to believe, there was no lack of spirit among them, despite their enormous losses.

It took time to mop up the entire region of Lippstadt-Paderborn, secure the area, and establish medical tents and sufficient prisoner facilities. Our companies were sporadically busy with various minor skirmishes and other duties, but by the third of April we were mostly on standby.

The crews of Company I spent most of our time on first echelon of maintenance, which is military lingo for routine and preventive maintenance, such as taking the engine's "vital signs"—checking oil levels, water, belts, replacing spark plugs, checking the tracks, and general inspection. Back in armored basic training, all tankers spent a considerable amount of time in motor pools, cleaning tanks and maintaining them and basically doing what we were now doing. Almost as bad as having your tank knocked out by an 88 or a Panzerfaust was having it break down at a crucial moment in combat, an occurrence all too common with Sherman tanks.

We had time to fraternize and banter with different crews in the company, getting to know our immediate comrades, men we had to coordinate our combat movements with. I met Staff Sergeant Shane Kelly, one of our tank commanders, who was said to be in line for a field commission. He not only had an excellent record but had been cited for his heroic success in leading a group of paratroopers through enemy lines to safety in the hedgerows of France—an achievement you were more likely to see among infantrymen than among tankers. Field commissions were uncommon and were the only way an enlisted man could become a commissioned officer without going through Officer Candidate School.

Sergeant Kelly was medium height, black haired (with some gray), affable, and a close buddy of Joe's. It was more important for tank commanders to know one another than for ordinary crewmen. It was the tank commanders who worked together and coordinated company battle movements. Kelly had been with the 3rd Armored since Normandy—the only soldier I met who had made the landing on Omaha Beach. The casualties at that landing are legendary and were, to me, incomprehensible.

On the fourth of April, we engaged in very little local combat, though the background noise of gunfire and artillery continued intermittently as various units were mopping up. Pete told me, as we stood smoking behind our tank, that Ugly had been wounded by shrapnel and was probably out of the war for good. A "million-dollar wound," it was called.

"How'd you like a million-dollar wound, Pete?" I asked.

He inhaled deeply on his butt and—I don't know how he did it—never exhaled any smoke. He looked at the mud surrounding his boots and said, "Y'know, I never gave that a thought. I suppose there's a bullet out there somewhere with my name on it. Maybe it'll kill me, maybe not." He shrugged. Then he looked at me with a faint smile. "What about you?"

"I don't think so," I replied.

"Meet a nice army nurse," he grinned, "get a little nooky, maybe."

I shook my worldly-wise head. "The price is too high."

I liked Pete. We seldom got chances like this to gab about stuff, and he was a good listener. He was frugal with his talk but always seemed to have something sensible to say. And I liked his looks, even the scant blond hair and three-day stubble. His somewhat high voice at first seemed all wrong for his huge frame, but it came to seem as natural to me as the sky above.

Joe came around the tank and joined us.

"What's goin' on?" Pete asked him.

"We're stayin' put till sometime t'morrow. Rumor has it we're on our way to Berlin. Goddamn, I hope that's right. How 'bout it, Pete. Berlin! I always wanted to see that city."

Pete nodded. "Yeah. That's the end of the fuckin' war, buddy— if they last that long. They can't have much more they can throw at us." He paused and stomped his cigarette butt into the dirt. "It's been a long, dirty road, Joe, but it's gotta have an end. The road can't be *that* long."

The supply train arrived, and we loaded fresh ammo into the turret, filled our monster's gas tanks, and stashed fresh rations on the back deck. The mail truck showed up, too, and we had a mail call. It was the first mail I'd got since I left Stolberg. It was better than Christmas. I quickly looked through my letters to see who had written. Amazing! There was a letter in there from Ruthie Collins, Rudy's sister. He must have written to her about me. The envelope was covered with thick kiss marks, leaving so much lipstick on the paper that it had smeared. I knew at once that I was deeply in love and should begin thinking about my future when I got out. One from my sister, Dot, one from my dad— which I opened up immediately. How's Mother? I wanted to know.

No one but a GI away from home, especially in a combat zone, knows what it's like to get mail this way. But mail call isn't always completely happy. There are disappointments, like no letter from Kitty, with whom I had supposed I had an "understanding." We would both be true to each other till "Jackie" came marching home again, hurrah! hurrah! Couldn't believe she had forgotten me. Must be something else. None from my brother. One from Mark Maston, my best buddy, who was in the navy.

Suddenly, things got quiet with guys sitting all around reading letters, once in a while letting out a whoop or a curse. No matter what, this tiny contact with the home front changed the weirdness of our present existence for a few moments, allowing us to continue to believe that the fighting had a purpose. And we got our PX rations—soap, cigarettes, aftershave lotion, blades and shave cream, hard candy, K rations, of course, and several packs of chewing gum. We tied a number of cases of "ten-in-one" rations (each sufficient for ten men for one day or one man for ten days) to the back deck. It was almost as though we had gone on vacation. What a lift in a moment of need!

The "water barrel" came alongside, and we treated our tank to a snort, filled our water cans, and grabbed a few minutes to wash what we could of our bodies and to shave. Pete grinned at me as he pretended to comb his scant hair. It really was like a vacation—too short.

The five of us stood by the tank and smoked.

"You married?" I asked Joe.

"Sweet wife and five li'l peppers."

"How 'bout you, Graver?" asked Pete. "You married?"

He scowled.

"Yeah, Ah'm married an' got three kiddies. But mah wife let me know that she wants a divorce when Ah get back. Ah don't know what's wrong."

Pete was married; Corkscrew was not. Pete proudly showed off pictures of his three kids—redheads, not surprisingly, all girls.

This was one of those rare moments when we could feel like ordinary human beings, talking together and discussing our private lives with one another and just engaging in guy talk.

About midday on the fifth we began moving eastward again

along four routes, with the two task forces of Combat Command A on the left (to our north) and the two of Combat Command B on the right. Our regiment was part of CCB under the task force of Colonel Welborn. We'd gone about four miles when our tank began to balk and sputter. It had to happen sooner or later. We had had good luck most of the time, but Sherman tanks, like the men who operate them, can get sick. Since we had just done maintenance, it wasn't obvious what was wrong. We lost about forty-five minutes trying to find the trouble, which turned out to be nothing more than some dirt in the carburetor. Meanwhile the columns moved on ahead. Our small misfortune was not unique, for we passed other Shermans with similar and even worse problems. It was a way of life with these machines, causing chagrin but nothing like having been knocked out altogether by enemy fire.

Despite the absence of serious resistance, we were not moving with any great speed. The Germans tried to control the speed of our advance by setting up frequent roadblocks defended by squads equipped with small arms, machine guns, and Panzerfausts. These delaying tactics were as hard on them as they were on us, for in each case they lost both men and weapons. They cost us time, of course, since there were too often prisoners to take with us and debris to clear away. The tendency on our part was to destroy both roadblocks and men. Prisoners were looked upon as anything but trophies at this point in the war.

Even as darkness entombed us all, our columns of armor continued the advance. All through the night we moved eastward, still encountering the occasional roadblock. Corkscrew had taken over the controls just before dark, giving Graver some much-needed relief. Graver had no booze to brace himself with, so he had to settle for plain, old-fashioned sleep in the bow gunner's hatch, noise and all. One thing a man learns in combat is that noise is nothing in itself and serves only to disguise the realities that threaten him.

We lost no tanks that next day, but a fair number of our armored infantry boys had been wounded or killed at various roadblocks. It was always hard to see one's comrades drop before enemy fire. And even though in the end the enemy is destroyed, one never forgets these tragic scenes.

On April 6, our columns were moving toward the Weser River, where, word had it, the bridges had not been blown—another false rumor, we were to discover. The Germans were putting up a surprising resistance. They were far from beaten, in their own minds. They were certain the Führer would not let them down. He, in their minds, no doubt had a grand coup de grâce prepared to be delivered at the right moment. So they fought with fanatical ferocity. Their troops were a conglomeration of remnants of the Waffen-SS and all sorts of other units that had retreated from Paderborn, as well as a few companies of "reserves," made up of old men and youngsters. All in all, they were mightily disciplined, and far too excellent soldiers to give an inch. But they had a weaker side, too, for they were virtually enslaved to their discipline. There was a close similarity between the way they fought and the way the British Redcoats fought in the American Revolution. They followed their battle plan to a tee, allowing individual soldiers and local commanders little room for personal judgment, often needlessly losing men and equipment. Their mechanical and predictable military behavior caused them many failures and casualties.

Captain Harkin radioed the information to the crews of Company I that we were to move up to the point of Task Force Welborn immediately. We moved ahead, passing the tanks of Company B, whom we were relieving. We were able to bypass several tiny villages, but several others were not so tiny and not so easily dispatched. The first of these was Hainholz, where a combination of ordinary infantry and SS commanders put on a display that surprised us, though we took the village in less than an hour.

At Borgholz our unit lost a half-track and half a dozen AI doughs. Clearing the village was not difficult. But Haarbruck was another matter. The resistance we met there was better directed and more sustained. Our tank's only threat came from Panzerfausts, but we saw a fair number of them. We were spared a near miss from one of them, which managed to disintegrate a large rock in front of us, allowing us to move on with ease. There was no German armor at all. But such observations never accurately tell the story. The enemy fought viciously, though in the end the streets contained more dead and wounded Germans than GIs. And I knew that behind the walls of the houses and in the cellars beneath them were frightened, cringing people, all fearing for their lives.

Our company suffered few casualties that day that I knew of, even though we met pockets of savage resistance. At one point, I was able to stick my head out of the turret hatch while Joe grabbed a smoke on the deck. It was no longer a novelty to see the immense destruction this war had brought to the German people. I could not think of them as the enemy, only the combatants. I wondered how the civilians could possibly survive in that rubble, how they would be able to feed themselves and their children. There were no stores, nowhere to buy food, clothes, or other necessities, and no way to escape the war. But I thought mostly of all those frightened children.

Joe had read my mind.

"Don't think about it, kid. It's a hell of a way to live and a hell of a way to die. Ya gotta tell yerself that you aren't the guilty one. Think about Adolf! Think about him! Think about what *he* did to his own people—what *he* did to all of Europe—what *he* did to the whole goddamn world! No sense in worryin' about anything 'cept gettin' it over an' gettin' home!"

I thought often about Joe's words. Every time I felt as though somehow it was my fault that I was killing people I didn't even know, I would remember them, and I clung to them like a moral life raft.

On the seventh of April the task forces had to halt. Apparently the Germans remembered their Remagen fiasco, where they failed in their attempt to blow up the bridge. Now they were making sure to blow up every bridge over every river no matter how large or small. This one was over the Weser River. It was a job for the engineers, who had the unenviable task of spanning the river under fire.

We were receiving indirect fire from across the river. It meant less to the men inside the tanks than it did to the engineers and the doughs, who were exposed. But although we were relatively secure in the Sherman, it wasn't a rest from the war for us, since we had to provide fire cover for the engineers. Still, there was a lot of waiting. The doughs of the 104th and 1st Infantry Divisions had the task of establishing a bridgehead on the far side of the river, and fighter-bombers were called in to knock out the German artillery harassing them.

Graver had somehow come upon a bottle of wine. I saw him

take a quick nip, then another, before sticking the bottle back into its hiding place. I saw where he kept it and couldn't help wondering how he managed to keep the bottles from breaking on the iron hull, what with the bouncing and jostling the tank provided. I could only hope that he would remain steady—assuming he was in the first place!

I had noticed that Joe was seldom inside the turret except under the heaviest fire. I mentioned this to Pete. It seemed strange to me.

"Well," Pete said slowly, "he wouldn't be happy with me if he knew I'd told you this, so you gotta swear to keep it to yourself."

" 'Course I will," I said.

"Well . . ." he hesitated ". . . Joe's got claustrophobia. Can't stand bein' cooped up in the tank, or anywhere else for that matter."

"Claustrophobia? Joe? Our tank commander? Our tank commander has claustrophobia?" I couldn't help myself; I started to chuckle.

"You promised, remember?" Pete looked a bit worried.

I swallowed a giggle.

"Don't worry, Pete," I assured him. "I'd never embarrass Joe—or you." I paused. "But it *is* funny," and I started laughing.

The engineers succeeded in bridging the river, and on the ninth we worked our way over the pontoon bridge, tank by tank, truck by truck, troop by troop, against steady enemy fire. Once we entered the bridgehead established by the infantry, however, we were able to pound back with mortars, direct cannon fire, and a blaze of small-arms fire. The outfit got across, only to discover a minefield on the other side. Our company lost a tank to a dreaded Riegel mine, but the boys inside were uninjured. Uninjured, that is, until a mortar round killed two and wounded two as they left the tank. We were not hit, but they were *our* men, from *our* company. And worst of all, we got the word that Sergeant Kelly was one of those killed. I believe the entire company felt a grief that only generated bitter determination and deep anger. There is no such thing as a glorious death in combat. There is only the helpless sense that "it could've been me." So much for the field commission.

We had to wait again while five doughs crawled through the minefield prodding the mud with bayonets. Pete explained that they were wiring the mines together as they found them to form a pathway through the field. Apparently they were able to connect the mines with wire in such a way that they could all be set off at once by a detonator.

"I've seen them do this before," he told me. "It's dangerous as hell out there. One lucky mortar round in the middle of the field and every one of those guys will be blown to bits. See how they crouch flat to the ground to make poor targets for bullets. And if one of the mines explodes prematurely, they'll all go off at the same time. Wiring is not SOP. Normally, they just prod the ground with bayonets and remove each mine."

"Why do they do it, then?" I asked.

"It's the fastest way to clear a path for us to get through."

The doughs succeeded somehow without getting killed, and then they detonated the mines, all at once. What a display! Rocks and mud went everywhere, raining on our vehicles and covering everything with a blackish-brown camouflage. The trouble we faced after that was having to pass single file through the minefield. No vehicles took the road for the first mile or so.

It was a given that the road was mined. We couldn't afford to lose another tank. Replacements were not coming up very quickly. And, of course, besides the mines, there was the slippery, boggy mud. Nothing new in that.

The First Army was moving eastward along four different routes, each route the objective of one of the combat commands. The strategy was simple: move along the fronts until enemy resistance required an offensive encounter. It was not considered necessary to completely secure every inch of ground as we went but to continue capturing ever new ground. By bits and pieces, I was gradually learning something of the immensity of the operation and figuring out which outfits were connected with ours. I seldom had the larger picture, so I felt some security in this knowledge of our extensive force.

We saw German tanks being blasted by fighter-bombers from the air and by our own antitank fire. We were somewhere in the vicinity of Harste, and we just kept moving slowly on. Graver seemed to be okay, but I knew that if he was completely sober, it was only because he had finished the last of his stash. Corkscrew did a lot of whistling, head downward into the hatch. He claimed he liked the weird sound it made as the wind rushed over his ears. I was sure he had room for rent between his ears.

Our monotony was broken only by the small towns we came to, where we would fan out and attack whatever force had been left to detain us. In one village—I'm sure it had a name—we paused to disarm the Krauts who stood around with their hands on their heads. One of these eyed me, and with a smile spoke in perfect American English—not even a trace of an accent.

"Got a cigarette, buddy?" His teeth were bad.

Why not? I gave him one.

"God!" he exclaimed after he had taken his first drag. "You don't know how good this tastes to me right now."

"Who are you?" I asked dumbly.

"I'm a German-American. Born in Germany, grew up from age two in Detroit. Man! American cigarettes are the absolute best."

I noticed his rifle stuck in the dirt, barrel down. He had no intention of ever using it again.

"How come you're in the German army?"

He frowned.

"I made a serious blunder. I came over with my mother in 1938 to visit some relatives, but somebody—one of my cousins, I'm sure—reported that I was a German citizen. That's all it took! They drafted me then and there."

Joe heard his story.

"Where'd you live in Detroit?" he asked.

And when he heard the answer, Joe grinned. Joe was from Detroit and knew the neighborhood this man had grown up in.

"I think we oughta take this guy with us. He can't be *all* bad. Wanna join the U.S. Army?"

The soldier exposed his bad teeth in a grin. "Why not?"

No way, of course. So I gave him the rest of my pack. He looked all around to see if any of his Kameraden had noticed. Then he looked back to me and pretended to hand me back the cigarettes.

"Danke, aber Ich rauche nicht sehr viel," he said loudly with a light toss of his head—all the while palming the pack as smoothly as any magician I've ever seen.

Taking prisoners always involved delays until headquarters

could send men to bring the prisoners to the nearest cages. Consequently, by midafternoon, doughs from the 13th Infantry Regiment took over, allowing us to move on.

Late in the afternoon, we came to another river—it looked more like a creek to me. This time we lucked out: it still had a bridge across it. It may have been a creek, but we still needed a bridge. The doughs secured it for us and prevented the Germans from blowing it up.

Every time I saw the infantrymen in action I rejoiced that I had escaped their ranks. It was only because I had done a stupid thing and ended up on my back for six weeks with a badly burned leg when I was in high school. I was working for the Pennsylvania Railroad, in the Paoli car shops—night shift on weekends during school; days, full-time, in the summer. We were cleaning the ten jillion small panes of glass of the shop windows one cold Sunday morning—around three A.M.—using, of all things, denatured alcohol and pumice. No need to go into details other than to say that I ended up with a seriously burned leg. I really suffered. And the ugly scar remained a flaming red for many months after I had recovered. Indeed, it was still hideous when I took my physical for the army in Philadelphia. And when the darling doctor asked me if I could walk any distance on that leg, I lied through my teeth and said no. He marked "B" on my report. I was a "class B" soldier. Only "class A" soldiers got into the infantry. Oh, what a heartbreaker!

Though I didn't envy those doughboys, I sure admired them. Without them there would be no war. Yet the guys I eventually got to know from the infantry told me they wouldn't trade places with me for gold. I couldn't quite figure that out, until a doughboy explained to me that tanks attract enemy fire, all kinds of fire. And when you're trapped inside a tank, there's nowhere to hide and no point in ducking. He'd seen enough tanks blasted and burned to favor a foxhole any day.

"Y'all may be safe from bullets and mortars, but ya cain't 'scape them shit-ass 88s!" one guy told me. "They come on like big-ass birds with a tailwind."

That gave me a new perspective, but I still felt safer with my tank.

CHAPTER 5

SMALL VICTORY,
BIG PRICE

The tenth of April was clear and warm as we traveled east toward the small town of Espchenrode, in the valley below the Harz Mountains. The signs of spring were disarming, and for once I saw no war wreckage defacing the landscape. I was glad to stick my head out of the turret and breathe the fresh air while Joe stood outside, leaning on the turret and smoking as we traveled. We were permitted for a moment to imagine that there was no war, that the world was, after all, a nice place in which to live—until we spotted German infantrymen in the fields.

"Get in your seat, kid, and get your sight on them. They probably just want to be taken prisoner. We don't need that, but let's not take a chance."

I climbed into the gunner's seat and swung the turret around to get them in my telescopic sight. The German platoon showed no sign of aggression, as they stood in waist-high grass. I watched for several minutes as we moved slowly on our way.

Then Joe called, "Don't worry about them, kid. We're gonna bypass them."

I was about to swing the turret back into the forward position when I saw two armored cars from the 703rd Tank Destroyer Battalion moving across the field toward the Germans. The Krauts immediately placed their hands on their heads in surrender. I was not surprised to see the armored cars turn around and begin heading back at that point. It was obvious that more prisoners was not what they had in mind. But as they pulled away, I could see the Germans duck down into the high grass and then rise up holding Panzerfausts and aiming at the retreating armored cars. Pete had already loaded the cannon with an HE shell. Without waiting for any command from Joe, I aimed at the Germans and fired, destroying the whole squad.

Joe had already turned away before I fired.

"What the hell did ya do that for?" he yelled at me uncharacteristically. "They only wanted to surrender."

I tried to explain to him about the Panzerfausts.

He just frowned at me. "I didn't see any Panzerfausts. From now on, kid, stick to protocol and wait for a command."

Joe was wrong, and I was depressed to have him angry with me. It had never happened before this.

The column continued eastward and then stopped temporarily. I just sat in my gunner's seat and waited, feeling low, while Joe continued to stand just behind the turret.

And then Captain Harkin radioed a message to the crews of Company I.

"I just received some strong praise from Colonel Showalter of the 703rd TD Battalion for our alert action that saved the two armored cars from the Panzerfausts. Whichever crew was responsible has my utmost thanks. Keep it up!"

The column began moving slowly again. Joe looked into the turret at me. I had just complained to Pete that I felt it was unfair of Joe not to believe me. Of course, Pete would have seen none of it from his position as loader, so he wasn't taking sides.

"Kid, do you smoke cigars?" Joe asked with a slight smile.

"I've smoked a few," I said.

He handed me one. "Keep it until you can enjoy it. It's a Havana. I only have—*had*—two." He paused awhile, then continued: "You did exactly the right thing back there. You made me look good, and I won't forget it."

I didn't give a damn about the cigar. It was Joe's words that rejuvenated me.

Our tanks and other equipment just behind us moved steadily toward the town. We were loaded and ready, aware that every village was a threat.

When the first tank got to the edge of the town, hell erupted in the road in front of them, but they managed to traverse the still-smoking hole and enter the town. We followed about fifty feet behind them and saw them take a hit from a Panzerfaust. The crew bailed out, all five of them, and crouched in doorways and alongside the walls of the houses, which were right on the dirt street—no such thing as a sidewalk. Intense machine-gun and bazooka fire came from the houses as doughs from the 36th Armored Infantry moved in and became entangled in a vicious house-to-house action. We maneuvered around the dormant tank and went along with them, blowing the walls out of houses for them to gain entrance, and giving them a cover of machine-gun fire. At one spot, Graver accidentally drove over the body of a German soldier. Miraculously, the track missed the wounded wretch, who was no longer our enemy and who needed someone's help. But then he was shot.

Without witnessing it, it would be hard to imagine the intensity of the fighting that went on in those narrow dirt lanes, where animals—dogs, chickens, even pigs—scampered frantically or became innocent victims like the civilians. Some of the homes had white cloths hanging from second-story windows to signal capitulation, as much as to say, "Please spare our home. We're not the guilty ones." Sadly, the white flags could not be honored, since those very windows often produced SS grenade launchers and machine-gun fire, and those very civilians were known sometimes to fire the Panzerfausts that caused us such awful casualties.

Corkscrew's machine gun jammed at one point and was out of action for a short while, until he was finally able to clear the chamber so the belt could be pulled out and replaced. He then proceeded to fire and jam the gun again. Perhaps it was defective ammo; perhaps it was defective Corkscrew. We also found ourselves caught in a "traffic jam" when a tank ahead of us was unable to make the turn at one of the narrow street corners, which were never intended to accommodate large vehicles, certainly not tanks. It was another of those unpleasant moments when we were not certain whether we were sitting ducks or battle reserves.

Then we were hit on the right sponson by a Panzerfaust that

penetrated the right gas tank. Joe didn't have to give an order. We just bailed out and ran for cover. Our tank was in flames.

We watched from our crouched positions against the wooden wall of a house. I never understood how metal tanks could burn until I realized that it wasn't the metal that was burning—it was everything else, including our barracks bags, rations, rubber on the tracks, grease, oil, and gasoline. And suddenly our ammo! We could feel the concussion from where we crouched. I was transfixed by the scene. In spite of the disaster, it seemed almost glorious! For that brief moment I was watching a war movie and feeling a thrill. But only for a moment.

Pete moved close and hollered, "We think Corkscrew is still in the tank."

"He can't be!" I yelled. "He'll be burned alive!"

Pete just looked at me, and I felt sick.

A war does not share your sorrow or your pain. An insignificant little German town was captured at a very big price. How many people—civilians and combatants alike—were destroyed that day I'll never know. But for us, the immediate problem was that we had no tank. We no longer had a weapon or a reason to be here. In fact, we no longer had so much as a means of defending ourselves; I had no weapon of any sort. Joe, for the first time since I had known him, looked despondent, staring at the smoking remains of the tank and kicking the wall of the house.

"Sorry, kid. I'm really gettin' tired of this war." He stood that way for several minutes, then looked up at me wearily. "We'll get another tank."

I was feeling all sorts of anxiety.

"Will we stay together as a crew?" I asked.

"I guess not all of us," he muttered half audibly, looking at the smoldering M4 that had been our home and was now Corkscrew's grave.

I couldn't even pronounce the name of the place. Espchenrode? We endured three years in that place—every hour was a year. But when the fighting was over, every last German soldier was either killed, wounded, or taken as prisoner. None escaped to fight again. Too many civilians, however, were also injured or killed—including children and babies. Some of those who survived would have been better off had they not. And little could be done for them until the medical units could move up. Our company lost two tanks that day. I never found out how many of our doughs were killed or wounded.

There had been six companies of crack troops led by SS officers, and they quit only when they were totally beaten. The little town of Espchenrode had been mostly destroyed, its blood-spattered streets littered with debris and military junk and dead things. And we were without a tank.

We just stood around, not speaking, soaking up the horror all around us. The medics of the 45th Armored Medical Battalion arrived and began picking up some of the living casualties and treating others where they lay. German prisoners were being herded toward the trucks that would take them to containment pens in the rear. Defeat had taken the military stiffness out of their demeanor as they straggled along with their guards.

Three replacement tanks were brought up from the rear late that afternoon. One of them was a Pershing M26 heavy tank with a 90-mm cannon, a model recently introduced to this war. We had trained in them at Fort Knox, and in gunnery school we gunners had been assured that this 90-mm was America's answer to the German 88. This particular tank, however, turned out to be the only one of its kind in Europe. We were told it was a Super Pershing and had been in action before. Its 90-mm cannon was longer than standard Pershing cannons; plus, it had two recoil cylinders mounted above the gun and considerable additional armor. It seemed strange that they should assign it to us, since we weren't even a full crew anymore without Corkscrew.

Graver wondered how difficult it would be to drive, considering the extra armor, and I was curious about handling this larger gun.

But Pete was unfazed. "Don't worry, we'll get used to it," he said. "We'll have more firepower and better protection."

We heard of one miracle that day, however. Captain Harkin relayed the information to us.

"PFC Korstue managed to survive the explosion," he said quietly. "He's in critical condition, badly burned. He's alive, but he won't see combat again. How long it will be until we get a replacement for him is hard to judge. You men have done an outstanding job. You'll be shorthanded now. Just give it your best. And take care of that tank!" He started walking away, stopped, then turned and said, "Oh, one thing more. The colonel reminds us all that there is to be no more looting. Seems some people have complained about things being taken from their homes. The rule is *no looting*!" Then, half under his breath: "And if you do any, see that you don't get caught!"

I thought about Corkscrew. His was not a "million-dollar wound." I knew something about burns. I had really suffered the time I burned my leg. The pain at times was beyond normal endurance. Without morphine I couldn't have stood it. I had no idea of how extensive Corkscrew's burns were, but it had to be most of his body. I could imagine his suffering. It was astonishing that he had survived that blast. It would be miraculous if he lived to tell about it.

We were without an assistant driver, but we were still a crew. We didn't have much time to get acquainted with our new machine. Compared to our old Sherman, this Pershing was spacious, had newer radio equipment, and the .50-caliber machine gun on the turret was more accessible for Joe. It would be easier for Graver to see through the wider slot on the driver's hatch; he wouldn't have to do his turtle act quite so often. I raised and lowered the gun and rotated the turret left and right and quickly decided that it would be easy to get used to.

Graver had no trouble driving. He admitted that despite its great weight, this tank was not any harder to drive than the old Sherman had been. But once again he somehow came into some "vino," and once again Joe had to threaten him with a "field court martial" with his .45.

"Ah ain't drunk," protested Graver. "Look! Bottle's nowheres near empty. Ah liked to died when we got hit. See my hand? Steady as ever."

It was trembling like an aspen leaf. Joe just scowled.

"Look, Graver, you're not used to this tank. I can't afford to have you all fucked up with booze at a time like this. Gimme the bottle!"

Reluctantly, Graver handed him the bottle, and he smashed it on the hull of the tank.

"Consider yourself christened," Joe muttered, looking at the tank.

It was dusk by this time. I was hungry, thirsty, and tired to the bone. My uniform, like everyone else's, was filthy and smelled pretty bad. And now we had no duffel bags, no change of clothes at all, including underwear. Joe managed to get us fresh rations—some K rations, a carton of "ten-in-one" rations, even some cigarettes. And we were able to grab some sleep; nothing else much mattered at the time.

Sleep usually entailed some guard duty. Graver woke me up sometime during the night to stand guard on the tank. I climbed up through the turret hatch, and got a whiff of cigar smoke.

"Where do you get those things?" I asked Joe, who seemed to be wide awake.

"My father gets them for me. Sends a box at a time. Pop knows cigars."

We stood beside the turret in silence, both exhausted.

"Joe," I said, "why don't you get some sleep?"

He shook his head wearily. "I'm tired, kid, but I can't shut my head off." He turned to me. "Go get some more sleep. I'll be here."

I draped myself over the turret and pretended to go to sleep. Joe sat by the turret on the tank deck. Within minutes, I could hear him snoring.

All was quiet, and I finally succumbed to my fatigue once again. I slept for an hour or so and then awakened to the sound of tank engines revving up. Joe woke up, too.

"Sounds like we're about to move out," he said, rubbing the coarse stubble on his chin and face.

"Graver!" he called. "Let's make some noise!"

I climbed down into the turret and yelled for Graver to wake up. Pete opened his eyes and growled.

"D'ya have t' make so goddamn much noise?"

Engines revved in Combat Command B, which comprised two armored task forces, Welborn and Lovelady. Our regiment was part of Colonel Welborn's task force. The entire command began moving eastward along the assigned routes, meeting no resistance as we went. This quiet, however, was not altogether welcome, for we all knew that the longer we went without resistance, the worse it would be when we met it.

The intensity of combat diminished any normal sense of time we had. Rarely did I know what day of the week it was, let alone the date. The weather had closed in, and a chilling drizzle made the landscape as dreary-looking as we felt. I couldn't keep my mind off Corkscrew, and realized that I missed him more than I ever thought I would. It would be hard on Graver, with no assistant driver to relieve him. But Pete agreed to take over if Graver needed relief—at least until we resumed combat.

Several times our column stopped while some elements encountered resistance. At each stop I closed my eyes and tried to shut it all out. Even when we were witness at one point to an engagement about a mile away between American TDs and a pair of panzers, I felt somewhat impassive. Three weeks earlier, I would have watched with wide-eyed wonder, but today it was just one more wearisome encounter. I found little excitement in it. Perhaps it was my colossal fatigue; perhaps I had become combat-hardened. Both, of course, were true. I closed my burning eyes and dozed.

"What's on your mind, kid?" asked Joe. He had been watching me.

"Nothing much," I answered. "It never seems to stop, does it? It just goes on and on."

Pete was in the loader's compartment. "Wish I could say you were wrong about that," he said, staring blankly at the distant fray through his periscope. "You're discoverin' what Joe and I know, that for every German tank or combat unit we wipe out, there's another waitin' its turn. You're right about it. Most of the time it seems there is no end. Best thing to do is to try to block it out of your mind as best you can and do what you have to do to stay alive."

"Well, there has to be an end," Joe offered. "We just don't know when we'll see it." Joe paused. "It's a way of life for now. Right, Graver?" he called.

"Ah'm listenin'," he replied weakly, "but nothin' you say makes it any easier."

Several depressing moments passed, and then Pete shouted, "Hey! Did ya ever hear the one about the lady who got hit by a bus? No? Well, it's in Dublin and this young woman tried to cross the street. See? But a bus came around the corner and hit 'er. Knocked her way up in the air, and when she came down she was stark naked, lying on her back. Well, you can guess *that* drew an audience. A circle of people—mostly men, of course—stood around her, gawking. A priest comes along, pushes through the crowd, and when he sees the unfortunate young woman lying naked in the street, he removes his hat and places it over the pubic area, to protect the lady's modesty.

"Now, about this time, Callahan stumbles out of the pub across the street. He's had a couple of pints beyond his limit. Callahan staggers across the street and pushes his way to the front, to see what it's all about. After a minute or so, he looks up at the priest and says, 'Father, seems to me the first thing we gotta do is get that man outta there.'"

I lost control, laughing hard enough to fall out of my seat. I thought Joe would collapse down from his perch onto me. Even Graver laughed—first time I ever saw him do that.

Funnier yet, a couple of the doughs on the deck were close enough to hear it and lost control laughing. One of them repeated the joke to the others, and suddenly the air was filled with raucous laughter. The guys on the tank behind us saw these howling hyenas and started to laugh, too. And *they* hadn't even heard the joke! It had to be a good five minutes before the hilarity died down. Humor and laughter are a great antidote to low morale.

The radio crackled in Joe's headset, and I heard him say "Roger!"

He had to use the intercom to talk to us, since engines all around us began revving up again.

"Captain Harkin just got orders from CCB for us to move to the head of the column," Joe explained. "They want heavy armor up front."

Even though I was behind all this firepower and reinforced armament, I felt a quiver in my stomach. Our diminished crew would be leading the entire combat command. The lead was an unenviable position under the best of circumstances. The tank was responding flawlessly so far. A group of doughs from the 36th Armored Infantry, who weren't laughing now, were riding on the deck, ready to jump off when their turn came.

The road was narrow but fairly straight, so Joe had a good view ahead. Suddenly I heard the roar of .50-caliber machine-gun fire above my head. Joe had spotted some Germans with Panzerfausts crouching in holes along the left side of the road. It was a standard trick of the Germans. Dig a line of holes as deep as a man's armpits, put a Panzersoldat (a German armored infantryman) in each hole, crouching down out of sight, and as the tanks pass by, they stand up, take aim, and blast away. It was a very simple but effective tactic and had put many Allied tanks away.

Joe couldn't tell whether he was hitting any, for they kept their heads down. Then, as we started passing the line of holes, the doughs on the deck began shooting systematically into each hole with their M1s to make sure every one was killed. Experience had shown that some of the Panzersoldaten would fake it until subsequent tanks were alongside and then jump up and fire. The doughs made sure that this did not happen to our tanks.

"That's a hell of a gun!" Joe exclaimed as he secured the .50-cal. "Ya need cotton in your ears when you shoot it."

He was right. My ears were ringing.

We moved on for about twenty minutes, when Joe ordered Graver to stop. I could see him scanning ahead with his field glasses.

"Looks like some kinda roadblock waitin' for us," he said. "Can't make it out. Doesn't look like any we've seen before."

"What's it look like?" Pete asked. He was straining through his periscope.

"Well, it seems like a wide stone wall of some kind stretching from about fifty feet from the left side of the road to fifty on the right. Can't be sure, but it looks like the top of a tank in the middle—can't be—it's not high enough."

"Could be a dismounted 88," Pete offered.

"We're gonna move on them. Let's go, Graver!"

I watched through my telescope, and as we got closer I could see what Joe was talking about. I got the gun in my sight.

Joe estimated that we were about half a mile from them and gave me the order, as Pete slammed a round of AP into the breech.

I set the sight and pulled the handle trigger. I could see a huge flash as it hit the gun turret. Strangely, the 88 did not fire.

"Stop the tank, Graver," Joe commanded. "Something's wrong up there. I smell some sort of trap."

Pete was peering through his periscope and said, "My guess is they aren't behind the wall at all. They've got an ambush set up on either side. They'll probably let us crash the wall, and when enough tanks are in range they'll let us all have it."

Joe got on the radio to Captain Harkin and explained what was going on—or not going on.

The captain said, "Hold on! I'll get back to you."

In less than two minutes Captain Harkin told Joe that Pete's guess was probably right.

"Just hold your position for the moment. We're moving tank destroyers in. There'll be two TDs on each side of the road, each accompanied by a large force of AI doughs. They'll be moving toward the wooded areas, where we're pretty sure the Krauts are located. Wait for an order."

We waited. About five minutes passed, and then I saw the TDs moving slowly over the terrain along the woods on both sides of the road. With them were the armored infantrymen, crouching as they followed.

The radio crackled again and Captain Harkin gave the order for Joe to move ahead very slowly, all crews being ready to give support as needed. And as we moved, I could see the TDs on both sides approach the woods. The doughs, including the guys who had been on our deck, were ready to go into the woods when the moment was right.

We moved slowly ahead, waiting to see if we would be needed. The TDs halted and began firing a constant barrage into the woods as fast as their guns could be loaded. From the woods came not only machine-gun and bazooka fire, but also 88 shells. One of the TDs on the left was hit and was on fire.

The order came for us to move down to assist those on the left, the tank behind us to move on the right, and the rest of the column to hold their positions.

As we moved our tank across the muddy field, its extra-wide tracks kept it from sinking into the mud as our old tank might have done. Joe directed Graver to a position just to the right of the burning TD. It was obvious that no one had survived in that crew. The doughs had infiltrated the woods, so we did not dare to fire our cannon in that direction.

It was hand-to-hand combat for the infantry. We continued to wait for at least half an hour, unable to see the fighting, though we could certainly hear it. When I saw infantrymen straggling out of the woods, it was clear that the battle was over but not clear what the outcome was. A few moments later, however, on both sides of the road, large numbers of Germans began to appear, hands on heads in surrender. We learned later how close those GIs came to defeat; casualties were extremely high.

Darkness began to close in as we moved back onto the road, taking the lead. A small group of combat engineers cleared an opening in the stone roadblock in front of the dummy tank. It turned out to be a genuine turret and gun removed from a defunct panzer, but it had no firepower and no gunner. During the

Civil War such a gun would have been called a "Quaker gun," a dummy to fool the enemy.

The order came for us to hold our positions and get some rest. We'd be moving out before daylight. My tenseness and anxiety dissipated into a much-needed sleep. I knew nothing whatever until the early dawn order came for us to move out.

CHAPTER 6

A LESSON
IN DEPRAVITY

There is no way under God's heaven that any of us could have been prepared for what the eleventh of April presented to us when we entered the city of Nordhausen. Nordhausen was the location of Germany's major assembly plant for the infamous V-rockets that had rained so much destruction on London and were expected eventually to reach even to Washington, D.C. What we saw there changed the whole way we thought about the war. The weather was cloudy, damp, and chilly—downright depressing. But the weather's mood perfectly reflected what we encountered in this place. By the city lay a camp that contained the barracks for slave laborers. The camp was known by the SS as Lager Nordhausen. General Boudinot himself entered the camp with the first tanks. Our tank was among them. There was virtually no resistance here, and it immediately became clear to us why we had met so much resistance at Espchenrode.

The first thing that greeted us were hundreds of semi-living men wearing filthy, ragged, striped prison uniforms, some standing, some crouched and trying to comprehend what was happening. And then we saw the dead and dying, lying naked in rows and heaps that reeked of human putrefaction. The stink of rotting human bodies impregnated my nasal passages, indelibly imprinting them with its sickening fetor. That hideous smell was something I will never forget, no matter how long I might live. This incredible stench made breathing a chore and brought us all to the point of nausea.

At one end of the camp hundreds of dead bodies were stacked, naked, like cordwood ready for the fire, and many hundreds more were lying in the parade ground between the barracks, laid out as though prepared for some sort of macabre full-field inspection. Yet worse than the dead were the half-dead, men who understood what was happening but were too weak to rejoice.

Also standing around the perimeter were SS prison guards, their weapons in the dirt in front of them, their hands on their heads. The report of several rounds of rifle fire indicated that some GIs couldn't control themselves, and General Boudinot gave the order to cease fire. Two Nazi guards had been killed, even though they were surrendering. The rest appeared ready to grab their weapons again to protect themselves.

"These are German prisoners of war," shouted General Boudinot, "and we treat them as such. The next man to fire on an unarmed person will be in violation of the Articles of War and will be summarily executed! We are *not* like *them*!" he shouted, pointing to the SS guards.

At that point, those prisoners who could came toward us,

smiling as best they were able. General Boudinot was surrounded by a group of them who tried fruitlessly to hoist him to their shoulders. We got out of our tanks and, despite the nauseating odor, started to wander around the compound, gazing in horror and disbelief. The air was filled not only with the odor of putrefaction but also with the moans of the half-dead creatures who attempted to greet us with the only sounds they could muster. We had not, at that point, even begun to grasp the extent of the horror we were to discover.

Other elements of Combat Command B came upon the actual factory in Dora, a village several kilometers to the north of the Nordhausen camp. It was here that Germany was constructing its infamous V-1 and V-2 rockets, as well as the newer V-3. And those who did the building, the slave laborers, were Hungarians, Poles, French, Belgians, Russians, and German "enemies of the state." It was discovered that the special prisoners who worked on the V-3 rockets had been shot to death in order to protect the secrets of the weapon. Nordhausen provided the barracks from which the workers were marched daily to Dora to toil long hours, beginning at four A.M. and ending late at night. They had to subsist on a daily allotment of four ounces of black bread and thin soup. The factory at Dora comprised two large parallel tunnels excavated in a hillside and extending underground for nearly two miles. A network of tunnels interconnected with these. The main tunnels were crammed with the machinery used to make the rockets. From what we learned later, Hitler had called off work on the atomic bomb—he considered it a "Jewish project" and much too time-consuming—and ordered full concentration on the V-bombs.

Our company was not at Dora and learned of its special

horrors only later. There was a crematorium at Dora that was unable to keep up with the dead, who were stacked there, as in Nordhausen, naked in heaps. But other heaps of human carcasses were partially covered by dirt, where bulldozers had been attempting to bury them before they were discovered.

At Nordhausen, a few of the prisoners talked with us in their various languages and with all manner of arm movements. Yet somehow we were able to communicate. We shared cigarettes with them and offered them some of our K rations (which may not have been a good idea—some got sick and threw up—though they were grateful just the same). I personally felt a bit embarrassed at the way they kowtowed to us and treated us as divinities. But the wonderful part was that we could tell them, over and over again, that their horror was over, that they would be getting medical attention, showers, and food. No more war! They learned *that* English very quickly.

"No more war!" they kept repeating.

True for them, but not for us.

We learned of their beatings, sometimes for no reason, and the bestial treatment they received on a daily basis, some purely sadistic, some homosexual attacks, and some as punishment for who-knows-what.

The whole experience of Nordhausen was incomprehensible to me. I had thought that I'd already seen all the abominations war had to offer. I now realized that the depths of savagery war produces cannot be exhausted. There will always be yet another atrocity, another shocking experience to extend my knowledge of how far human beings can go in their own moral degradation. I had not been a proper student in high school, yet I knew that I was becoming educated about the world far beyond the scope of a high school diploma.

Nordhausen and Dora did more to create in me a desire to suppress my memories of this war than anything I had seen or would see. Like so many other young men in the war, I wanted to find a gloss that would hide what I knew could never be hidden. How could I accept the fact that human beings like my father and my mother—like myself—could in any way be a party to such evil? How could such decent people *make excuses for it*? I had been taught that God forgives sins of every magnitude, but how could any "loving Father" forgive these crimes? Perhaps I would someday forget this place, but at the moment I couldn't imagine how. Seeing, smelling, hearing all that atmosphere was like entering another world altogether. I could not then, I cannot now, comprehend this dimension of human depravity. And one day I would learn that this was only "the minors"; I never got to see "the majors," the big-time death camps at Auschwitz and Buchenwald and the like.

We were still in the camp when the division commander, General Doyle O. Hickey, came to see for himself what had been radioed to him. He slowly shook his head as he took it in, chewing the stem-stub of his pipe. He and General Boudinot walked slowly through the area as medic "meat wagons" were gathering the worst cases among the sick for transport to medical facilities a few miles to the rear. I watched the general to see how he would react. I was not surprised to see him put his handkerchief to his nose against the stench.

I saw Graver bending over beside the tank, vomiting profusely. I went over to him and placed my hand on his shoulder. He stopped vomiting, but his body trembled. He remained in a kneeling position, hand to his forehead, and sobbed.

"Why are we here?"

I helped him to his feet. Something was happening to him. He took the New Testament from his pocket and threw it in the mud, then climbed up into the tank. I watched as he pulled the hatch closed and I picked his New Testament from the mud, wiped it off, and stuck it into my pocket. Perhaps Graver would have second thoughts. So far as I know, he never did.

The picture was never complete. We saw fourteen-year-old boys, and men aged beyond their years and dying of tuberculosis, dysentery, and starvation. Some were still able to manage the daily walk to Dora for work. But as I looked around, I saw no healthy ones, and I wondered how the Germans were expecting to build these bombs with such a broken-down workforce. I never found a proper answer to that question, except that there are always more people to enslave.

GIs were everywhere, wandering and trying to talk to prisoners, offering them cigarettes and items from their rations. It was not long until members of the 143rd Armored Signal Company arrived and began photographing everything before it could be cleaned up. And meanwhile, the Nazi guards continued to stand along the perimeter, not so stiffly now, but still with their hands on their heads. AI doughs had collected their weapons, and I saw at least one GI put his face up to a guard and blow cigarette smoke slowly and deliberately in his face.

There never seemed to be a final horror to discover. In the unlit barracks, where a number of us ventured, a different smell mingled with what already filled the air. Piles of human excrement and pails of urine in various places indicated that sanitary facilities had never been a part of this camp. Most of the beds were boards with filthy rags or pieces of clothing to cover them, serving as sheets and blankets. Most of the prisoners had not even had that luxury but slept on the dirt floors. Evidence of unbelievable cruelty was everywhere in Lager Nordhausen. These people were treated—used—as if they were not human; as if they were merely expendable sources of labor. That and nothing more. The dogs kept by the guards never received such treatment as these human beings.

I approached the guards, walked slowly in front of them, and looked into their faces. I had expected to see twisted, ugly, vicious countenances but saw instead mostly handsome, unrepentant young men, some no older than I. There were, of course, many other guards in other parts of the camp and at Dora. There was no way to estimate their number, though it must have been in the hundreds.

When the command was given for all troops to return to their companies, I found Joe standing with his hands on his hips, just staring.

"C'mon," he said. "We gotta get back to the tank. We're gonna spend the night on the edge of the city. This human cesspool is a place to forget, not to remember."

World War II was in black-and-white with shades of gray—no trace of the Technicolor that transformed Dorothy's movie-Kansas into Oz. Even though spring had slipped in on us—more or less—it had no power to brighten our combat world. Nordhausen became for us a passage from seeing war as simple destruction to grasping its ever-latent depravity. The world, it seemed, could never be normal again, perhaps *we* would never be normal again. But it was not as though we were finished with war; we had merely reached the nadir—or so we hoped! Even in the heat of combat, one used to hear GIs banter profanely, sometimes even making tasteless jokes about the destruction all around them. But not now, not here.

Many of the citizens of Nordhausen denied any knowledge of the camp and the factory. In fact, they vehemently denied that there was such a place. It was nothing more than Allied propaganda. "Germans are Christian people and would never engage in such atrocities," they insisted. They acknowledged that there was a work camp for enemies of the state, but nothing as vile as the Americans claimed. And, incredibly, they seemed to believe what they said. Only after large numbers of them had been walked through the camp to see for themselves would they finally believe what they could no longer deny.

We mounted our tanks and moved to an assembly area in a field on the east end of the city of Nordhausen. Captain Harkin visited each crew of the company. He was no longer the threatening authority figure he had been to me not so long ago, for I had since come to see him in an altogether different light, the semilucency of combat. He came over to our tank, helmet in hand and running his fingers through his slightly graying hair.

"It's a hell of a business," he said quietly. "Look, you men're getting a replacement for Korstue. He'll be here sometime soon, I hope this afternoon. How's the tank working out?"

"Okay," Joe said. "We're getting used to it."

He looked at me. "Have you used that gun yet?"

"Yes, sir," I said. "And I'm really impressed."

"I should think so. You men are doing a good job."

He gave me a faint smile. "Not a hell of a lot of glory in all this, is there?" he said and walked away.

No one would be able to tell his rank merely by looking at him. None of the officers wore their rank on their uniforms, not in combat. Just a white stripe on the back of the helmet and helmet liner. And the captain's uniform was almost as filthy as ours. His combat boots were shabby and mud-covered, but he was, in spite of that, trim in his appearance and bearing. He had contacted Supply and reminded them that we needed fresh clothing—"But don't hold your breath," he had told us.

I couldn't tell how many of them there were, but the Nazi prison guards were being herded by twos in a long column west of Nordhausen, on their trek to a better life in a U.S. prison facility. If they were lucky, they would end up in the States in some army prison camp, where they would lie and say that they were completely innocent of the terrible things "the others" did. Life for American-held POWs was a pretty good deal, for the most part.

We spent the night in the assembly area and got some much-needed sleep. I felt truly sorry for Graver. He was not cut out for this life. I suppose few of us were, but Graver seemed to suffer from the whole combat thing more than most. Yet I admired the way he managed to keep up his part of the job.

The night was too short, and early on the morning of the twelfth, tank engines were already roaring, and Joe nodded to me to mount up. Pete was checking the ammo in the turret floor, the radio was crackling off and on with various communications, and Joe got into his seat in the turret, his hatch open. This Pershing, for all its bulk, was actually less noisy inside than the old Sherman had been. We waited as several doughs climbed aboard for the ride. And then we were off, Graver driving and not looking entirely well.

The sun rose behind thin clouds, and once again we played follow-the-leader along the disintegrating remains of a macadam road. The mountains were flattening into mere foothills as we headed eastward toward the next engagement, whatever it would be. I kept my eyes glued to the small 360-degree prism "window" available to me in this tank. Occasionally I would use the periscope, which could be rotated. There was nothing special to look at, but it gave me some satisfaction to see the world outside. For some reason, I thought about Smitty and wondered how he would have reacted to Nordhausen. I had a fantasy that he was with us while we were back there, and he got into a temper and wanted to kill every German he saw. The fantasy, of course, was really mine, and "Smitty" was my own personal outrage and frustration at something over which I had no control and which I couldn't quite comprehend.

We were not the lead company as we moved out on the twelfth, which suited us fine. There was usually enough fighting to go around for all to get their turns. Our column stopped around midmorning, while the city of Sangerhausen was being captured and cleared. We played the part of reserves, ready to move up if needed. We had time to eat, smoke, and banter about home and fried chicken. I saw Rudy Collins standing by a tank up the road, and decided to compare notes with him.

"You told your sister about me," I grinned. "Thanks. She sent me a love letter."

"Don't let it go to your heart," Rudy warned. "She writes letters like that to all the guys. She has the dumb female idea that she's making all these GIs happy so they can fight the war better. Just enjoy them, but don't take them seriously."

That was not what I wanted to hear.

"You're a real morale-buster, Rudy," I grumbled. "It was love at first read for me. What d'ya think? How 'bout if she saw me in person? Think I'd have a chance?"

He scanned me up and down, as though he were buying a new car.

"Well, put it this way. Seein' as how she's not even eighteen yet . . ."

The order to "Mount up!" was being relayed down the column, and I hurried back to my tank. Tank engines revved and roared and we were on the road again. Pete was driving now to give Graver a break. With no assistant driver to share the load, Graver really needed a rest. Things were tough for him without a little "vino" to ward off the devils of this frightening world. Before long I dozed off in the gunner's seat. I don't know how long my nap lasted—fifteen minutes, maybe.

The column stopped again. Replacements had caught up to us, riding in two half-tracks. The four of our crew stood by the tank, watching to see what sort of guy we were getting. Lieutenant Miller from Company B came along the row of tanks, parceling out the replacements. When he reached us, there was only one left, a very short, dumpy, freckle-faced, red-headed PFC.

"Gentlemen," said Lieutenant Miller, looking at his list, "this is PFC Sean Irvin, your replacement. I think we're up to strength now."

Sean Irvin apparently didn't know how to smile. I reached out my hand to him, but he ignored it.

"Everybody calls me 'Shorty' for some damn reason."

I pulled my hand back. I wasn't sure what to make of this guy, so I didn't rush things. I'd let him find out that my name was

Irwin from someone else and that we'd be getting mistaken for each other, since nobody pays any attention to such details as the difference between a *v* and a *w*.

Joe chuckled. "Can't imagine why. This is T5 Graver, our driver, and Sergeant Kowanski, loader. Corporal Irwin here is our gunner. You'll be assistant driver–bow gunner. Seen any action?"

He shook his head. "No, I'm a rookie over here. Been three stinkin' years in tanks, though. Stateside. Cadre at Fort Knox. They're really scrapin' the barrel when they send piss-ass runts like me over here."

"We got nothin' against runts here, piss-ass or otherwise," Pete said with a grin. "We just need a crew member. Regular army?"

"Me?" he croaked, grabbing his throat as though he had a chicken bone stuck in it. His multiple chins wobbled when he talked. "Me—regular army? Me, who spent two of my three years goin' AWOL tryin' to avoid the army? No ma'am, sister! I only let them send me over here because the goddamn war is practically over."

Practically over! How can it be practically over, I thought, when we keep on fighting day after day? This guy was amusing.

"What're we workin' with?" he asked, gazing at the tank. "Pershing M26. Looks different somehow."

He walked around the tank, looking it over.

"It's been retrofitted," I said. "A custom job. Lots more armor and a longer cannon."

Shorty pushed out his lower lip. "That's a hell of a gun. Looks pretty long, all right. Wouldn't want to be the Krauts up against that thing."

"Guess you haven't seen a King Tiger, have you?"

"Only pictures," said Shorty.

But pictures don't fight back. I had high hopes for this machine against German armor, but only time would tell. So far, I gave it top marks.

Though we weren't the lead company, as we moved out again it seemed clear that we would be involved in the next encounter. This turned out to be a nameless little dorf, nameless to us at least. While its defenses were small, its defenders were as determined as any others. It was around noon when the first elements arrived, and within half an hour we were called up to join the fray. A number of the tanks were having mechanical trouble, due to a lack of 50-weight oil. We had been advancing too rapidly for supplies to keep up. Our own crew, however, was fortunate so far in not having any problem, so we moved up.

The German forces here were prepared for us with the usual Panzerfausts, heavy machine guns, mortars, antitank artillery, and determined troops. While there was no way the town could hold out against our forces, we nevertheless did not have an easy time of it. I got the chance to use the big cannon against a barricade defended by an antitank gun surrounded by sandbags and accompanied by infantrymen who were laying down a barrage of machine-gun fire against the infantry. A round from the AT gun ricocheted off our reinforced front armor.

"That was lucky, kid," yelled Joe. "Answer them with HE!"

My shot fell short, but the blast it made in the ground in front did some damage to the barricade.

"Again!" shouted Joe.

As Pete loaded the shell, the gun from another tank knocked out the AT gun.

"Save the ammo!" Joe called, so I held my fire.

We moved slowly into the town with the doughs, who did most of the fighting. At the street intersection ahead of us, I saw the doughs dash for cover. When we arrived, a panzer was facing the intersection on the street to the right. I started to rotate the turret toward it, but Joe gave the order to hold off. The panzer appeared to him to be a dummy.

That "dummy" tank turned out to be far from lifeless. As we slowly approached, it fired at us and hit our front turret plate. Had it not been for the added armor, it probably would have killed all three of us in the turret—Joe, Pete, and myself.

"Hit 'em, kid!" shouted Joe.

And I did, right at the turret base. It appeared that the round penetrated to the interior, and within a few seconds we saw the turret hatch open and a man, accompanied by smoke and flames, climbed out. Only one. The panzer, we learned, had in fact been disabled, but the gunner—alone—tried to man it as both loader and gunner. My God! What guts! After it was all over and this gunner had been taken prisoner, I had a chance to talk to him, something very rare for us. He spoke some English and explained what he had done. I couldn't help myself—I reached out my hand, and he took it, smiling through the grime on his face. We shook, and for a moment we were just comrades in battle. I was glad we hadn't killed him.

It was not, however, a time for fraternizing, and I quickly returned to my tank. Fortunately, Joe understood what I had done and why.

"I'da done the same," he said quietly.

We waited while prisoners were rounded up by the infantry, which gave us time for a couple of smokes. Some civilians came out of their homes to inspect the wreckage. There were lots of tears and wailing, something I could never get used to. I climbed into the tank so I wouldn't have to see them. Why, I wondered, did these insignificant little places have to suffer such damage? The answer was, of course, because the German command selected them as part of their delaying tactics. In this case, as in others, it was Wehrmacht infantry, rather than professionals like the SS and other elite elements, who had the assignment. These Wehrmacht Soldaten were, like us, mostly draftees—good fighters but lacking the discipline and fanaticism of Hitler's "Aryan" forces. I had the feeling that they were expendable in a way the professionals were not.

It was late afternoon, and the sun was getting low in the west. Supply trucks arrived bringing us gasoline, some heavy oil (though not enough), rations, and other supplies. It was difficult for them to get through to us, since we moved so fast that many areas remained unsecured, and they were harassed by machine-gun fire, Panzerfausts, and the like. They often had to drive the trucks through gauntlets at top speed, hoping to get through without becoming casualties. They normally wore .45-caliber pistols, and some trucks had machine guns for emergency defense. However, they depended mostly on their skill as drivers to get through, and many lost their lives in the process. They were truly combat soldiers, even though they didn't actually fight. We couldn't have survived without them.

The order came to move out again. The intent had been to reach the Saale River before dark. After less than an hour, though, the column stopped again, and I Company was ordered to move up toward the head. We were widening our front as we approached the town of Eisleben. It was known that on the outskirts of Eisleben was a prisoner-of-war camp, but what sort of resistance we might run into was unknown. Happily, there was little, and the reward we got from the British POWs, in the form of cheers and waves, gave us all a much-needed lift. Unlike the prisoners at Nordhausen, these men looked human and reasonably healthy. These Brits had been POWs for a very long time, some since North Africa and Crete, some since Norway, and many since the debacle of Dunkirk. They wandered among our tanks and shook our hands, graciously accepting our cigarettes and generally looking us over as though we were divinities from a distant planet.

"Damn!" exclaimed one captain. "You chaps could reach from here to bloody Berlin with all this material!"

"That is one hell of a fuckin' tank!" exclaimed a corporal, his eyes sweeping our tank in amazement. "How big a fuckin' gun you got there?"

I grinned, with appropriate pride. "Ninety millimeters. It's supposed to be the Allies' answer to the Kraut 88. We just got this tank. Our old Sherman was a casualty."

He shook his head slowly in disbelief. "They come a long fuckin' way since I was a bloody crewman in North Africa."

I offered him a cigarette, but he held up his hand. "Don't smoke. It'll stunt yer growth."

This made me laugh. He couldn't have been more than five-one or two.

"Truth is," he continued, "I had a fuckin' bad chest wound. The medical bastards warned me that smokin' could be bad for my fuckin' health." He looked at my cigarette pack longingly, then reached for one. "Oh, bloody hell! One fuckin' fag can't kill me. I've already been bloody dead once."

This sort of fraternization continued until the Brits were

loaded onto trucks for free U.S. transport to the rear, the first leg of their journey to their own forces. Then it was eastward again toward the Saale, but eventually darkness stopped us. We felt no sorrow about this. Tomorrow was always out there waiting for us.

CHAPTER 7

ONE LAST RIVER

On Friday, April 13, we reached the Saale River. We were out of the Harz Mountains completely and facing flatter, more congenial terrain but here we were halted by yet another river, its bridges blown, of course. And once again there were German defenses waiting for us. I saw no armor, but a formidable array of antitank cannons were carefully dug in on a rise above the opposite shore. Besides these AT guns we could see numerous machine-gun emplacements. This would not be an easy crossing, especially without artillery support. The 391st Artillery Battalion, our usual support, was engaged elsewhere, since, despite appearances to us, the enemy force we faced was considered the "softest" section of the German defenses.

Task Force Welborn spread out across a wide front about a mile from the river. We received no immediate fire; they were clearly saving their resources for our river crossing. That crossing, of course, would depend on the construction of pontoon bridges. Consequently, the regiment established defenses at the crossing location to protect the engineers when they proceeded to build.

Our own company was at the moment up to strength. We stayed with our tanks, prepared to receive orders. Such times are always filled with a certain amount of dread, so it was not surprising to see Graver sneaking a quick nip. Shorty saw him and climbed out of his hatch and crossed over to Graver's. He could sense the man's anxiety.

"You wanta swap places with me?" he asked quietly. "A bow gunner only has one thing to take care of—his machine gun. Doesn't have to think about another damn thing except firing it."

Graver remained silent at first. Then he said, "Ah can't kill anyone. Ah just can't. Killin' someone is worse for me than gettin' killed. When ah shoot that bow gun, ah try to miss 'em. Ah'm no damn good here."

Shorty looked him in the eye and said, "You drive the tank so others can kill them. You're already as deep as anyone else here when it comes to killin' people. We're all part of the big killing machine, even the truck drivers who bring our supplies. Most of those Germans over there are gonna be killed or wounded tomorrow, some of them by this crew right here. What the hell difference does it make *who* the bastard is that does it?"

I overheard this whole conversation. I had underestimated Shorty. He gave me something to think about. But I wondered what effect his words would have on Graver.

Graver said nothing. He just sat in the driver's seat and stared ahead blankly. Shorty shrugged his shoulders and went back to his hatch. It was several minutes before Graver climbed out of his hatch and crawled over to Shorty.

"Ah know what y'all say makes sense, but when ah'm rasslin' with the controls, Ah don't think about anything else. Ah'm better off as a jockey."

Elements of the 23rd Armored Engineers were brought up to span the river. As always, it would be under fire from the Germans. Our company got the order to approach the riverbank at the bridge area and establish positions where we could give cover for the engineers. Almost immediately, we began to receive AT fire from the other side, and we began firing at their positions. We knocked out two of the ATs. The heavy machine-gun and mortar fire kept the engineers back from the river, behind the cover of rocks and rises. They automatically began digging their foxholes, for they would need them to retreat to as the Germans harassed them with heavy fire. The engineers then did what they often did—waited out the rest of the daylight in order to build during the darkness. I never quite understood how they did it. About 120 AI doughs managed to climb their way across the remains of the original bridge and establish a bridgehead on the opposite shore. They dug in and were ready to give fire cover against the Germans to help protect the engineers.

Pete made some quip about "Friday the thirteenth" and how we should wait for a better time. Joe heard him and snickered.

"If I didn't know you better, Pete," said Joe, "I'd think you were superstitious."

"Oh, I am! I am! I'm even afraid of a black cat's shadow!"

"The hell ya say!" Joe laughed.

A mortar round exploded about twenty yards away, and bits of shrapnel flew everywhere. Then another one hit closer.

"They're tryin' to tell us something, like, 'Get your asses inside, where it's safe.' So batten the hatches, boys," Joe shouted.

It was plain to see that the mortar fire was not really intended for us but was simply an attempt to get the range of the engineers so they could be bombarded after darkness. Nevertheless, a barrage of tank fire blasted away at the Germans. How much we accomplished I couldn't determine.

Tanks of Task Force Welborn were moved to positions of defense behind various shallow depressions along the slope above the riverbank. Here they would stay until dawn. The armored infantry doughs stayed close to the tanks, where they would have some protection and could easily be moved into action when needed.

All night the engineers worked as quietly as possible. Every sound brought small arms or mortar fire in that direction. Yet, almost miraculously, by earliest dawn, two marvelous pontoon bridges had been completed, and we lost none of the engineers. To us, it was a triumph; to the engineers, it was "just what we do! We're armored engineers!" Shorty was right. They, too, were part of our "big killing machine," though they didn't fire a shot.

At 0600 hours, tanks of CCB began the crossing on the two pontoon bridges. As expected, the Germans opened up with everything they had, and even as we were crossing, our crews fired back. Not one of those first tanks was knocked out by anti-tank guns, despite considerable fire from the other side. And one by one, those ATs were destroyed. It remained for us to wipe out the rest of the emplacements. That job, however, was more difficult than we'd guessed, for Panzersoldaten were well positioned to give us grief. We lost one tank to a Panzerfaust. The crew escaped, but the burning remains spread a cloud of dense black smoke over the whole area. Together, doughs and tanks moved through the choking smoke, which, despite its discomfort, served briefly as cover, long enough, at least, for them to get close to the emplacements. At that point a savage firefight took place.

Our own tank had crossed the river without incident, and we were ordered to add firepower on the left, where two more tanks had been disabled.

"Okay, gunner," Joe said into the intercom, "you can see them. Take care of 'em."

That meant not to wait for individual commands. Pete and I worked as one; he was a great loader and made my job easier. Joe was on the .50-cal., laying down some heavy fire. The American .50-caliber machine gun was high on the list of very effective small arms in this war. It was the envy of the German Army and the pride of the GIs. Shorty seemed to be enjoying his part as bow gunner; he was a great addition to our crew.

After an hour and a half, it was over, and we had losses: three tanks disabled and fifteen men wounded, two dead. The Germans, however, suffered rather more, for they were completely routed, and seventy-nine prisoners were taken. The story, as usual, was with the casualties. There were almost as many dead or wounded Germans as there were prisoners.

We lined up our tanks near the road. I watched as the wounded were being picked up by the 45th Medical Battalion, and I began to wonder about the dead.

"What happens to all those dead bodies out there, Pete?" I asked.

"The Americans lie there till the Graves Registration people come to pick 'em up," he said.

"What about the Germans? Who picks *them* up?"

"I'm not really sure how it works. I suppose there's some sort of arrangement between the two sides for exchanges," Pete replied, scratching his head.

I had more questions.

"Well, what about the disabled tanks and stuff?"

"Goddamn, you're full of questions." He grinned. "Ordnance tank retrievers pick up the ones that can be restored for combat. The others are cannibalized for parts. Any more questions?"

"Yeah, but they can wait." I smiled.

At about 1000 hours, Task Force Welborn continued the drive eastward. We were not the lead company, about which we had no serious complaint. A number of the tanks soon had to stop to add oil. No one knew how long it would be before supplies would catch up to us. Pete mentioned to Joe that we were down to about half-load with shells. There seemed to be plenty of .30-cal., and Joe mentioned that he had used more than half of his .50-cal. rounds. To make matters worse, marauding Panzer-soldaten attempted to sneak up on the tanks that were "separated from the herd" to blast them. Fortunately, in every case they were spotted, and we did not lose any vehicles.

Joe told us that the order had come for us to keep by our tanks, ready to move out within ten or fifteen minutes. To me, as to everyone else, the fighting seemed interminable, always another river to cross, always another battle to fight. There seemed to be no end to it. Joe, Pete, and I were standing on the deck, smoking. Graver and Shorty were standing together, leaning against the tank and chatting.

I asked Joe, "Was the fighting always this bad?"

Joe and Pete looked at each other without a smile between them, caught a bit off guard by my naïve question.

"Fighting is fighting," Joe replied. "It's always bad. Guys trying to kill each other any way they can."

"Yeah, I guess so," I murmured.

"One thing about it," added Pete. "It just goes on and on, and ya never think it's gonna stop."

"But sometimes it seems worse than at other times," I pressed. "Would you say it was worse in France and Belgium than here?"

"No way to compare it," said Pete. " 'Worse' is just the way you feel about it at a particular time. Some days it seems like it's the worst ever, even when there's not a hell of a lot goin' on."

"Combat is combat," repeated Joe. "Men always die. And you never get used to it. It's always something new."

"How can the Krauts keep it up?" I wondered out loud. "We're kicking their asses, but they just keep on fighting."

Pete flicked his cigarette away and gave me one of his stares of wisdom.

"Just suppose this was the U.S.A. and things were the other way around, the Krauts invading us. What would you do?"

"I get your point," I said. "Guess I could learn to be a fanatic, too."

And then we were moving again. The 3rd Armored Division was spread out along four routes moving toward the Elbe and Mulde Rivers. The two task forces of CCB, Welborn and Lovelady, were following a southerly route. Lovelady was to the south of us. We moved without incident and within half an hour we reached the Reichsautobahn, a dual highway, the first I had ever seen. Four concrete lanes, two going in one direction and two going in the opposite direction, separated in the middle by a median strip. Hitler ordered the Autobahn system for rapid transport of military equipment. And that's exactly what we intended to use it for. We used all four lanes as we headed for the Mulde. Against all hopes, by the time we got there the bridges had been destroyed, and we were stopped.

The Spearhead Division had outdistanced its infantry support and supply trains. Both the 1st and 9th Infantry Divisions were occupying the region around the Harz Mountains to secure it from recapture by the Germans. The 104th Infantry was heavily engaged in the Halle area, thirty or forty miles to the south. Consequently, a detachment of our 36th Armored Infantry was sent across the river to establish a shallow bridgehead. Our tanks had moved off the Autobahn onto a narrow paved road, where we soon encountered strong resistance. Our tank was hit twice in succession by small cannon fire from two armored cars. They were part of a mobile defense unit intended more for harassment than serious combat. I fired at one and disabled it. The other was hit by another crew, but it managed to escape nonetheless. Once again, our thick armor plate had saved us from serious damage.

We were less than ten miles south of the city of Dessau, and we were stalled as we waited for the engineers to bridge another river. This time, however, the Germans were determined not to let that happen. Even before the engineers were in place to begin, extremely heavy artillery and mortar fire showed us how resolute the Germans really were.

At this point in the war, the Germans were bringing together absolutely every possible resource, human and material. The common opinion was that they intended to make an all-out stand to prevent any further move toward Berlin. The division would thus stay put until every one of our units was up to strength. And that depended on supplies catching up to us. We spent our time in local skirmishes with various mobile German defense units. Although they always presented a threat and could cause damage and losses, our main concern was the expenditure of fuel and ammunition, which were already in very short supply.

"We're gettin' low on gas," Graver called from his cockpit.

"Can't do much about it," Joe shouted. "Try to conserve. Don't idle the engine any more than you have to. This monster uses too much gas as it is."

We had no choice but to collect the companies to proceed to various defensive positions until we were resupplied. Meanwhile, the engineers were under intense artillery fire from across the Mulde, making any progress on the bridge next to impossible. And even when they succeeded in getting a few sections in place, the frequent tree bursts—fragmentation shells that exploded in the air—sent fragments to puncture the pontoons. The artillery and mortar pounding was incessant, leaving the engineers little opportunity to do their work. I was beginning to wonder about our chances here. Maybe we would be stopped altogether.

"What's your problem, Jack?" Pete asked me. It was the first time he had called me by my name.

"Oh, nothing," I said. "I'm just thinking bad thoughts. I'll get over it."

"Well, if your 'bad thoughts' are what I think they are, turn 'em off. We didn't come this far to back off. It's not gonna happen. The fuckin' Krauts are puttin' on a show of bravado. They can't hold out."

I figured he was right, but when you're this low on supplies and don't know when refreshments will be coming, well, it's scary, to say the least.

The column of tanks moved toward the river and separated into various defensive positions. Company I was directed to a small farmhouse surrounded by perhaps an acre of ground. It was located close to a railroad embankment that more or less paralleled the Mulde about a mile or so on the other side. There we found room for all of our tanks and vehicles. The farmhouse itself, while still occupied by its family, served as company headquarters. Once we were lined up, Captain Harkin came out to explain our situation.

"Men, we're here temporarily until the rear units have caught up. There's almost no chance that we will be attacked. The Germans are depending on their artillery and mortar shelling to prevent a crossing of the river. You can stay with your vehicles, if you wish. If you can find a decent spot to rest, good. But, damn it, don't go wandering off anywhere. When the orders come, we have to be ready to move at once. Any questions?" None.

Captain Harkin and Lieutenant Wilson, his assistant, had their quarters in two rooms on the lower floor of the house. The kitchen was left free for the family to use. They also occupied the second floor. Still, the captain insisted on having several guards planted inside and outside the house to prevent a sneak attack of German infantrymen and to keep the family under observation, lest they somehow communicate information to the Nazis in some way. As a precaution, their telephone wire was cut and their radios were confiscated. This was probably not necessary, since there was no longer any telephone service or radio broadcasts.

The cellar under the house had a door from the outside but no access from inside. It was small, dark, and damp, an ideal place for a bunch of weary, smelly GIs, who opposed the idea of getting killed by artillery fire, to hang out. And that fire was almost constant, though the main target was the engineers and their aborted bridge attempt. I chose to sit in the tank and write letters home, although I had no idea when they would get picked up and sent. The rest of our crew were crowded in the cellar with the others. I had the turret hatch open and could hear the ripping noise of the artillery coming from across the Mulde. Suddenly, an artillery shell grazed the top of the railroad bank and passed harmlessly over the house. It occurred to me that we were safe here from the artillery. There was no way they could hit *us*.

Emboldened by this knowledge, I decided to crawl up the ladder into the barn and take a nap. From the cellar, Joe could see me.

"Irwin!" he shouted. "You asshole! You'll be blown to bits!"

"It's okay," I yelled. "There's no way they can hit us behind this embankment."

"You're an idiot!" came the reply.

In the barn loft, I started to make a bed with what straw I could find. As I lay on my back I could hear for the first time the familiar ring and hum of our own artillery heading across the river. I felt a great relief. Our rear units had caught up, and now we could enjoy some fire cover. I relaxed and dozed. But not for long. A tremendous explosion immediately outside the barn sent gravel and mud against the barn wall. After the millisecond it took me to decide, I was on my way down the ladder, scarcely touching the rungs. I raced to the cellar and jumped in amid raucous and mortifying laughter.

"Thought ya had it all figured out," yelled Joe.

"Guess I forgot about mortars." I grinned sheepishly.

Division rear elements had pretty much caught up with the main body—with the exception of Supply. We learned that German troops were able to harass the supply columns, destroying a number of trucks, effectively preventing them from getting through. It was one reason we were stuck at this point and could advance no farther. The other reason was the fact that the engineers were having so much trouble building the bridge. The German mortars and heavy shelling harassed them constantly. It was clear that the Krauts were determined that we should not see Berlin.

CHAPTER 8

PRELUDE
TO A FINALE

German artillery fire never let up against the stubborn engineers as they continued their efforts to bridge the Mulde. We were not getting very much at the farmhouse where we were stationed. I was leaning against the tank, smoking and daydreaming, when Shorty came over and stood beside me. He lit up a cigarette.

"You named Irvin, too?" he asked.

"Not quite. It's spelled with a *w*. But I've heard that it's all the same clan," I said cautiously.

"You from Pennsylvania?"

"Yeah. You?"

"Mauch Chunk. Ever hear of it?"

"My mother was born near there. Her father and brothers were all miners."

This information made an impact on him.

He looked at me with a frown. "What's her last name?"

"Harris," I answered. "Her father was John Harris."

Shorty removed his helmet and scratched his wiry red hair.

"I knew a John Harris. Friend of my father. Called 'Jack.'"

"That was probably my Uncle Jack. He was no taller than you."

He nodded, a slight frown on his face. "Imagine that. Small world."

The conversation was over, but he continued standing beside me, smoking. I tried to get a handle on him. Odd sort of duck. Seemed like a hothead before, but three steps closer to friendly at the moment. Well, I thought, I'm not here to make friends, but I want to get along with my crewmates.

Joe and Pete hurried across the compound with a sense of urgency.

"C'mon, you guys, we got a job. Shorty, you get in the driver's seat. Let's mount up!" Joe shouted.

"Where's Graver?" I asked Joe.

"Last I heard he'd found some cognac. We may never see him again, friggen lush!"

We climbed into our positions.

"Crank it up, Shorty. We're takin' a short ride up onto the street where we can get a view of that town over there."

Pete was loading HE into the breech as Shorty moved us onto the road. The high-explosive shells would do more damage to buildings than armor-piercing shells.

"This is good," said Joe. "Okay, kid. Can you see that church steeple stickin' up above the roofs of that town?"

I traversed the turret back and forth, my eye to the telescopic sight, until I spotted the church steeple. "Got it!" I called.

"Take it out!" shouted Joe.

"You mean . . . just shoot it off?" I asked.

"Damn it, yes! Now!" Joe was impatient. "Try it at seventeen hundred yards."

I did, but the shell was low and blew out part of the church itself.

"Kick it up to eighteen hundred," called Joe.

This time the shell just blew off the tip of the steeple.

"I think you got the range," said Joe. "It's up to you."

I dropped my sight a hair and fired again. One church in that town was missing a steeple.

"Now we have to do the same for every high peak or spire in the town. Do it!"

I spent the next fifteen minutes blowing up all the steeples and high points on every building in the town. It seemed to me like a senseless mission, but it was excellent target practice. When I was finished, Pete grinned at me.

"Nice work—and on Sunday, too. I'm not sure the man up there is happy with you," he said, pointing upward with his thumb.

"What the hell's this all about, Joe?" I asked. "Seems like a waste of ammo to me."

"You got a lot to learn, kid. We're pretty sure the Krauts had FOs in one or more of those high points, directing the artillery fire we're gettin'."

Forward observers! I hadn't thought of that.

"Hope we got 'em," I said.

"Don't we all," he answered.

FOs or not, the engineers were still getting intermittent artillery and mortar fire from across the river. Whenever there was a break in the fire, they went back to work on the bridge. However hopeless the job may have seemed to them, they stuck to their work, adding a section at a time, sometimes getting fired on before they got the section finished, sometimes losing a section to tree bursts. It was a heroic effort on their part. In many ways their job was even more dangerous than that of infantry and tankers, who could at least shoot back. The report we heard was that several engineers had been wounded. None killed.

Time began to hang heavy on our hands that afternoon, as we sweated out the intermittent incoming mail that was harassing the engineers at the Mulde River, which before long became the "Moldy River." I wrote three V-mails during the afternoon, including a very romantically suggestive one to Ruthie Collins. I figured she wouldn't take it any more seriously than she did her own letters to guys like me. It was becoming a game between us, and it seemed like more fun than the slobbery, worrisome, serious business of true lovers. And anyhow, I knew I'd never actually meet her again.

The division had moved so rapidly over the last weeks that our supply lines were unacceptably thin and vulnerable to enemy attacks. In fact, the route we had taken when coming to this place was through an extensive wooded area, ideal for enemy attacks on our supply trains. We kept hearing about losses of supplies, and we worried about our dwindling supplies of gasoline, oil, ammunition—even food and water. Scarier still was the state of our cigarette supply. It was low. Division brass had been attempting various tactics to eliminate the offenses against our supplies with some success. But there was one major forested area where the Germans were still cutting off our trucks, no more than seven miles from where we were located.

At 2000 hours Joe corralled the crew.

"We just got another job. The captain has ordered us to take the road back that we came on and blast the woods on both sides. There'll be three tank crews—us and Benson and Lynch. Us and Benson will blast to the right. Lynch will blast to the left."

"When?" I asked stupidly.

"Now, goddamn it!" shouted Joe. "Rev up!"

Graver was sleeping somewhere, still in his cups, so Shorty took over as driver.

"Move out!" shouted Joe. "Benson and Lynch will lead. We'll be number three."

Our tiny column of three tanks moved out in early darkness along the designated road, driving for a little over five miles, and on command we began firing straight into the woods lining the road. The woods were dense, and in the growing darkness we had no idea what or where our targets were. We would stop, fire, and move ahead. We unloaded volleys of HE shells, white phosphorus shells (of which we still had our full complement), and machine-gun fire into the dense forest, and before long the woods were ablaze.

I had the turret turned toward the woods, and Joe accompanied my cannon and .30-cal. fire with the big .50-cal. machine gun mounted nicely on the turret.

It seemed like a crazy mission. We just moved down the road for about ten, perhaps fifteen miles, firing into the woods and setting everything on fire on both sides of the road. Benson's crew swung their turret back and forth, firing into the woods on both sides. It wasn't clear to me what we were accomplishing by this action, but it was not up to me to decide. *Somebody* had to know what this was all about.

It was only after several hours that we finally returned to our area. Pete mentioned that we were entirely out of HE shells. We had only a few of the white phosphorus shells left and mighty little machine-gun ammo. Only upon our return did we learn that our mission had been intended to make it possible for the supply trains to get through.

It must have worked. The next morning Captain Harkin called the company together for the first "Fall out!" I had seen since leaving the "repple-depple" after we left Stolberg. He explained our mission and our success to the whole company. And he praised the hell out of us. I was not able to understand why; it had seemed such a simple operation. But according to the captain, we had accomplished what no others had in five attempts, namely, we had driven the Krauts out of the wooded areas, and our supplies could once again come through safely.

"I Company will be remembered for this," he stated, "and I want to personally and publicly give the credit to these three crews. As a result, we can expect to receive fresh supplies tomorrow."

That last news brought cheers and applause. For me, the captain's remarks had special meaning. They were another instance of the sort of validation I had hoped to hear from him the time I reported with my prisoners—that time so long ago when I was so sure I would be acclaimed a war hero. War is hell, of course, but it is also strange and paradoxical, not at all the sort of world in which sense and nonsense are easily distinguishable. Perhaps that is for the best, for the job of lowly GIs like me was to follow orders, whether they made sense to me or not.

The supply columns from Trains showed up that afternoon, April 16th, bringing ammunition, heavy oil and 100-octane gasoline in five-gallon cans for the tanks, food rations, cigarettes, some PX rations, including soap and shaving supplies, and, best of all—mail. Everyone got into the act, unloading supplies. The tank commanders apportioned them to the various crews. Then came the work of stocking the tanks, gassing them, adding oil and water as needed, and loading the ammo into the racks. Pete was slightly surprised that we actually got the right 90-mm shells for our big gun. In the end, all the tanks were up to standard and ready to roll when the command came. Then came the mail call and another of those moments that reminded us why we were here.

It was also on this day that we learned of the death of President Roosevelt, who had died on the twelfth. Lieutenant Wilson gave us the news, and none of us were sure what this would mean for the war or for the troops. But he assured us that our forces would continue as before, maybe fight a little harder to honor our late president. For most GIs, the president, as commander-in-chief, deserved high praise.

On the seventeenth, we had some free time, during which we treated ourselves to helmet baths and other such frivolous activities despite the perpetual shelling and damp, chilly weather. Manny Fredericks, a T5 from a different crew in our company, had been an army barber before shipping out to this place. His price was one pack of cigarettes. It was worth it, and he had all the business he could handle. He gave only crew cuts, however,

so the guys who had a narcissistic attachment to their lovely locks went without his services or suffered a tonsorial affront to their pride. Not surprisingly, his nickname was "Scissors."

It was not a time of rest and rehabilitation for us—anything but. The war was everywhere around us, and we continually heard reports of the fighting of other units. That day we learned that our companion task force, Lovelady, to the south of us at Thurland, was attacked by a force of German infantrymen—between one and two hundred of them. The predawn attack was carefully planned and flawlessly carried out. Our troops were billeted in the town, and the Germans fired bazookas and Panzerfausts into their billets. It was a day of heavy fighting for them; we heard about the savage battle that ensued lasting into the late afternoon. In the end, the German commandos were routed, but the little town of Thurland had been destroyed.

That evening, the order came from Army Command to halt all attempts to bridge the Mulde, much to the relief of the bone-weary engineers. Had they persisted, sooner or later they would have finished their bridge. But as it was, the change in plans didn't hurt their feelings a bit. The infantrymen who were dug in on the bridgehead across the river were recalled. It wasn't clear to us what our next move would be, but the rumor factory was busily grinding away. One rumor had it that Russian shells were already crossing the Elbe and that there would be a joint American-Russian attack on Dessau. That one turned out to be false; there never was to be any such "joint" operation. Another rumor claimed that the Russians were already in Dessau. Again false. The Russians were still miles to the east.

Another more plausible rumor had it that Dessau was to be the focus of our next attack. Hope started running high among the men—like a wildfire fanned by the winds of rumor—that this would be our last encounter with the enemy. The anticipation, however, was a mixture of anxiety and fear as well as hope. No one wanted to become a casualty so near the end, to buy it on the last day of combat. And there could be no doubt that there would be a great many casualties, for Dessau was known to harbor fanatically determined remnants of earlier campaigns as well as crack troops from the Rosslau-Dessau school of combat engineering. Large remnants of various SS combat groups, determined to halt the march on Berlin by the Americans, had arrived as reinforcements.

Tension began to fill the air. With nothing to go on but conflicting rumors, most of the men waited out the time with little chatter. An occasional chuckle or whoop merely meant that some of the men were occupying their minds with other things. But all around the company compound an atmosphere of apprehension collected around the men like a ground fog. Despite the fact that most of these men had been through much heavy fighting already, there seemed to be a sense that this next battle would be somehow different, although no one knew in what way.

Graver showed up, looking like he'd been run over by a tank, and Joe gave him a talking-to.

"Look, Graver," he said quietly, "it's no mystery why you booze it up. I can understand it. None of us is really cut out for this kind of life. But we need each other in the tight spots. A drunken tank driver can be worse than no tank driver sometimes. I need your hand that you won't touch another drop of booze of any kind until we're finally out of this. After that, you can booze yourself into oblivion if you want. It won't be my grave. What d'ya say?"

Graver looked ashamed and extended a trembling hand to Joe. They shook on it.

"Ah guess y'all think Ah'm pretty worthless," he muttered, his eyes looking at the ground ahead. "Ah wanta do my part, it's just that . . ."

"Take it easy," Joe said, reassuringly. "You're not worthless, Graver, just frightened, like every guy around here. You've proven yourself many times in combat. You're a damn good tank driver— when you're sober. We'll be needing a good tank driver like you when we're at it again."

"And after that, how long's it gonna be? There's no end to it."

Joe put his hand on Graver's shoulder. "There's an end to it, buddy, and it's not far away. Believe me, it ain't gonna be long."

"If we survive," Graver muttered solemnly.

Lieutenant Wilson came out to where most of the men were standing, sitting, or lying on the damp ground. He circled his arm and shouted, "Company!"

The men gathered around to get the briefing. The lieutenant confirmed the suspicion that Dessau would be our next objective. He wasn't sure exactly when.

"But it won't be more than a day or so," he concluded. "I'll keep you informed as we learn more details." He started to walk away, then turned and added, "Oh, and tomorrow we'll be moving outta here. Colonel Welborn has ordered all units of the task force to assemble in an as yet undisclosed area. You'll hear more tomorrow."

So at least some of the rumors were right. Dessau, a large city on the juncture of the Elbe and Mulde Rivers, had become the collection point for the last major stand by the Germans. Tanks, armored cars, Panzersoldaten, antitank guns on panzer chassis, and heavy infantry could be expected. Hitler was in his bunker in Berlin, so the American forces must be stopped at all costs. We could only hope to overwhelm them with an attack force way beyond their expectations. Yet, in their minds, there was no force they could not stand up to for the Führer.

The next day, Wednesday, April 18th, we received our orders to move out to the designated area, where the rest of the task force would be gathering. We were the first company to arrive, but we were soon joined by the others with their tanks, half-tracks, peeps, and other vehicles. We were directed to areas set aside for our various companies and attached units. Our instructions were to stay with our tanks for the time being. Then at 1200 hours we were to be served a hot meal in a large mess tent now being set up.

This last was the best news we had heard yet. I scrounged in my barracks bag for my mess kit, which I hadn't used in quite a long time. I hunted and hunted, but it soon became clear that it wasn't there. I mention this to Joe.

"You have a short memory, kid," he said. "Remember Espchenrode?"

"Oh, yeah," I said. "Damn it to hell!"

We had been issued new barracks bags after our tank had been destroyed, but no such niceties as mess kits and utensils.

"Don't worry," said Joe. "You'll get something to eat. You're not the only duck without feathers."

Our whole crew stood together by the tank—smoking, of course. Joe had only one cigar, which he was saving for the right moment, so he settled for his Luckies. There was not much to talk about, and none of us felt very talky anyhow. Pete chewed on his cigarette, as though he couldn't wait for chow.

We heard the music at noon. "Chow! Line up!" It sounded almost like the good old days of basic training. We entered the mess tent, and on our right was a crate full of mess kits and utensils.

"If ya got no mess kit, take one!" yelled the mess sergeant. "If ya do, don't take one. They have to go around."

We went down the mess line just the way we did back at Fort Knox. But somehow, this chow looked and smelled better than any I had had to date. Beef in gravy (from cans, we knew), little boiled potatoes (also from cans), mixed vegetables (these were no exception), fruit cocktail (ditto), and the first hot coffee any of us had had for a long while. To us it was a gourmet feast. It's incredible how something so simple as hot food can raise the morale of weary combat soldiers. We had been living on boring cold rations for months. It was good to hear lots of voices and laughter again. We were going to be all right. Uncharacteristically, there was almost no garbage to toss in the GI cans outside.

We could hear artillery fire from the south, and twice I saw groups of P-47 Thunderbolts heading in that direction. This was no "cooling off" period—quite the opposite. The fact that I could see the whole task force collected in one area gave me a feeling of confidence. Combat Command B had been ordered to maintain a defensive position from the village of Torten, not far from where we were located, to the village of Raguhn, about six miles to the south. All the while, bitter fighting went on in various villages, mostly within a ten-mile radius south of Dessau.

The nineteenth of April was a day of waiting for orders, and just waiting in general. There was not much for us to do but stand around, smoking and talking. The mess tent had been taken down—that was a one-shot deal. Joe was talking with Sergeant Tony Field, another tank commander. Graver was stretched out on the back deck, asleep. Pete, Shorty, and I leaned back against the front of the tank, trying to think of something other than combat. Shorty talked about some of his escapades as a cadreman at Fort Knox and had us laughing. I told about one guy in my platoon who was bucking for a "Section Eight" and who went to incredible lengths to convince the army that he was nuts. One of his worst stunts happened on the grenade range.

"Pigg—that was his name—Pigg was on the practice grenade range. He was known as such a fuck-up that the lieutenant in charge of the range stood right in back of him. Pigg was a right-hander, but he had his grenade in his left hand. He stepped up behind the barrier, pulled the pin from the grenade, and threw the *pin* over the barrier, dropping the grenade on the ground behind him. The lieutenant grabbed the grenade and threw it over the barrier. It went off in the air, and a tiny piece of shrapnel tore through the lieutenant's ear. Pigg found himself on company punishment for a week."

Shorty smiled and Pete laughed a little.

"Sounds like a guy I knew," said Pete. "He was a sleepwalker. Well, one night, he—" He got no further. Joe came over and told us to get our stuff packed on the tank and be ready to roll.

"We'll be leaving here tomorrow."

CHAPTER 9

THE ROAD
HAS AN END

The orders came on the evening of the twentieth to prepare to move out at 0400 hours tomorrow. Task Force Welborn would take the route north, keeping the Mulde on our right. You knew it was coming, but you're never ready when it does. I tried to get some sleep; it would be a long day tomorrow. I put my bedroll under the tank and crawled in it. For a while my mind kept turning over, but eventually, I got to sleep. But 0400 hours came pretty fast, and I got up, pulled my bedroll from under the tank, and tossed it onto the tank deck.

I ate a box of K rations, and washed it down with water from my canteen. A lousy breakfast. Graver, looking a bit more like himself, was already in the driver's hatch. The rest of us got into our seats. Pete looked over at me.

"You're nervous, aren't you, Irwin?"

I hated that he could tell. "Yeah, sort of. Not too bad, though."

"C'mon," he yelled, "I'm nervous as hell. I'm pretty damned scared! How could you *not* be worried?"

I felt relieved. "I guess I am scared a little."

He grinned a comforting grin. "That's more like it. Face your fears the way you face your enemy. Ya gotta fight 'em both at the same time."

Pete was one guy I felt I could love like a father. He seemed so savvy and sensitive. With him as our loader, and Joe at the helm, I knew we'd be okay. Graver? I always felt sorry for him. It can't be much fun to have to suffer his torment. And I had a hunch that Shorty Irvin had ice in his blood; he'd just do whatever had to be done.

We moved out—tanks, half-tracks carrying boys of the 36th Armored Infantry, trucks carrying supplies, and somewhere behind us was the 703rd Tank Destroyer Battalion. It was more than an hour before we reached the outskirts of Dessau, and already we were taking mortar and artillery fire from German artillery. Clearly, the Germans had no intention of handing the city over to us. But they, too, were receiving heavy fire from the 391st Armored Field Artillery Battalion, just to our rear.

Graver surprised me. I knew he was scared to death, yet he didn't let it prevent him from doing a good job. That, I thought, was heroic about him. He certainly wasn't a hero at heart. Joe had once told me that in combat there are only cowards and liars. The difference between them is that although the cowards may survive, the liars win the battles. And, he added solemnly, only the liars can be heroes.

"A guy has to lie to himself that killing and destroying aren't wrong, and that he's not really afraid."

With these thoughts to shield my moral sensitivities, I prepared myself for yet another battle.

Task Force Welborn was one of four task forces joining in a four-pronged attack on the city. TF Hogan was attacking directly from the west; TF Boles and TF Orr were moving in from the southwest; we were driving from the south. As we approached the city, our way was blocked by Panzersperren, concrete tank barriers that were difficult to destroy. Our tanks were unable to climb over them or break through them. They had to be destroyed. Since there was no time to wait for engineers to do the job, we used our tank cannons to blow them up. It was slow and tedious and required the expenditure of valuable ammunition, but eventually we were able to make openings at various locations sufficient for the tanks to move through. We continued our advance on the city.

Dessau had been taking punishment from artillery and air strikes for several days. As we approached, the city appeared shrouded in an eerie, hazy fog, a mixture of smoke and the thin cloud cover already dimming the early sun's rays. Unlike on our approach to Paderborn, we were not greeted by attacking armor, which told us that the German stand would be purely defensive. They had no benzene to spare, and we knew that what they had would have to suffice, for there were no supply routes open to the city. Dessau was a city under siege.

We had learned much about the German will and determination by this time. We had learned, for example, that they were trained not to think about their weaknesses but only about their superiority. And, unfortunately, despite Allied successes, a certain mythology persisted among GIs that German technology had produced tanks that were almost invincible. I had heard this view in advance of my first contact with German armor, and it had worried me greatly. But my own experience proved the myth to be exactly that. On the other hand, I could not free myself of a fear of the giant Tiger, Germany's awesome heavy tank. I knew of its firepower and heavy armor. But I had also learned of one of its weaknesses—its slow turret traverse. Unlike our Shermans and Pershings, the Tiger had a manual rather than a power traverse. It was a weakness I had learned to exploit. And I got my chance all too soon.

Our tanks entered the city slowly and spread out along different streets, alert to any sudden appearance of German firepower. The half-tracks behind us stopped, and the armored infantry doughs dismounted and began to move with the tanks. Fortunately, Pete had loaded our cannon, for as we turned the corner onto a street, we were confronted with a Tiger, and it was ready for us. The gunner fired at us as we rounded the corner, but missed us completely. The shell went high, over our tank. I returned fire point-blank at the royal monster, but saw the tracer of my shell ricochet off the front armor and take a course of its own skyward. Pete slammed another round into the breech, and at that same moment we heard a thud on the turret. But I took aim and fired again, and this time the shell penetrated the thin armor on the Tiger's exposed underbelly as it attempted to climb over some rubble. The ammo, located in the turret floor, exploded, leaving the burning hulk of the Tiger obstructing our path.

We had been hit, but there was no evidence of serious damage.

"Just keep going," Joe said into the intercom. "Great shot, kid."

The fight for Dessau, like the fight for other towns and cities, involved mostly house-to-house combat, which meant that doughs and tanks worked together, moving slowly down the streets until fired upon. Again it was Panzerfausts and bazookas and machine-gun fire from windows and doorways. The infantry also had to be on the watch for snipers from the German combat engineers of the Rosslau-Dessau school, each one an expert marksman. Their rifle fire was as deadly at times as machine-gun fire. It was not an easy time for our infantry, but they gave as good as they got. Our tanks had to be forever on the lookout for German armor, which was sometimes dug in and sometimes marauding.

I was called on to blow out the fronts of houses from which enemy fire harassed us, giving our doughs clear entrance. In some blocks we progressed literally house by house. We lost quite a few men—wounded and killed. Medics from the 45th Armored Medical Battalion, who were unarmed, seemed always to be nearby and able to get the wounded men to safe places where they could treat them. Not often, but occasionally, a medic became a casualty. A medical corporal once told me that a part of their training was the art of survival under fire. "Timing is a big part of it," he said. It was mesmerizing to watch them at work—never knowing when they would be fired upon yet not thinking about it.

Many of the streets of Dessau were cobbled, often narrow, and sometimes graced with narrow stone archways that spanned the street. Some of these archways were already damaged by tanks—both German and American—attempting to squeeze through. When we came to one of these arches, Graver hesitated.

"What'm Ah s'posed to do now?" he called on the intercom.

Joe estimated that the tank would scrape both sides and probably get jammed.

"We don't want to take a chance," Joe replied. "Turn around. We'll take another street."

We had no map of the city with us, and were Joe not in constant communication with Company Command, we would quickly have become hopelessly lost. Graver did as ordered, but we suddenly came under fire. Panzerfausts!

"Stop," Joe shouted, and Graver did, just as an explosion erupted in front of our tank.

We knew the fire was coming from somewhere to our left rear. I turned the turret in that direction.

No more fire came our way. Joe decided that we should save our ammo and move on.

"Graver, turn this thing around and move as fast as you can back down the street."

We encountered a great deal of smoke from burning houses and from gunfire. In some places it was so bad that it was almost impossible to fire on targets without endangering our own men and equipment. Making matters even worse, large numbers of Germans were staggering or limping or just plain trudging through the smoke waving handkerchiefs or whatever white rags they could produce. At one point I had to stop firing because I couldn't tell the combatants from the surrenderers.

An order came for us to hold our position until further communication. This we did, but not peacefully, for we were constantly under fire from Panzerfausts. They appeared to be coming from a single direction. How we escaped being hit was a mystery to me. The answer came, however, when I saw several of our doughs come from a house with two children at gunpoint, a girl and a boy. They could not have been more than ten or eleven years old. They did not wear the uniform of the Hitler Youth. My guess was that they had been trying to hit us with Panzerfausts but had had no training. It was more evidence of German desperation.

The command came for us to move to the next street, the one to our west paralleling this one. The order was to "clear that area," which meant doing exactly what we had been doing. We did as ordered and received no fire of any kind. The doughs crouched in doorways or stuck close to the tanks, expecting the worst at any moment.

"Keep ready," said Joe over the intercom.

It was eerie. Perhaps "spooky" is a better word. By all appearances, this street was not harboring any of the enemy. Then, in an instant, it seemed that every window on the street had all manner of gunfire and bazooka fire spewing forth. A number of our boys were hit and lying in the street and on the sidewalks.

"No more sweetness and light!" shouted Joe angrily. "Blast every window and building on the block! Give these fuckin' bastards something to remember!"

We moved along the street, systematically blasting every house front as we went. I was using HE shells, to cause as much destruction as I could. Joe blasted away with the .50-caliber machine gun, and Shorty was firing his .30-cal. into every window he could see. Pete slammed a white phosphorus shell into the breech and yelled "Phosphorus!" at me. I fired, and the effect of the shot was devastating: a fire broke out in the building I had hit and before long had begun to spread to the adjacent buildings. Our firepower and the heavy rifle and automatic-weapon fire from the doughs made it possible for the medics to do their work. They moved from casualty to casualty, determining who could be helped and who would be left for Graves Registration.

As more and more Germans surrendered, their sheer numbers started to impede our movement. We had joined several tanks of our command, and one tank commander—I didn't recognize him—yelled at the Krauts in German, warning them to get the hell out of the way or get run over. Then he ordered his driver to move on. It was like the parting of the Red Sea! And we all followed in his wake. Miraculously, no Germans got squashed—they had gotten the message.

In late afternoon, a rumor spread that Germans had knocked out one of our tanks and murdered the crew. According to the story, the Americans stood together next to their helpless tank with their hands on their heads. Without warning, the Germans opened fire on them at point-blank range, killing all. Such things did happen, and the rumor was taken as fact. The result was that many of us were outraged and felt like retaliating against the surrendering Germans. We were held in check by wiser, calmer veterans. Joe and Pete had heard the tale, too, and seemed to give it less weight. Joe saw how upset I was.

"Don't let it get to you," he said. "We're in a war. Keep that in mind."

"Yeah, but that's plain murder!" I exclaimed. "That's not combat!"

"Maybe they thought it was," said Pete. "Maybe in their near-hysterical state they were thinking, 'The only good American is a dead American.' Truth is," he added soberly, "we're as guilty as they are! We've murdered a few ourselves."

I guessed I still had not been around this war long enough not to be outraged, although it seemed to me I'd been here forever.

Our unit was ordered to halt where we were and stand as reserves. That gave us a chance to smoke and stand idle. Aching fatigue forced us to doze where we stood. My eyes burned from the smoke that was everywhere in the city, and I was by now so tired I didn't even want anything to eat.

Suddenly Shorty, who was in his seat, opened up with his .30-cal. bow gun. He fired several bursts.

"What the hell're you shootin' at?" Joe shouted. He looked where Shorty had been shooting and saw two Panzersoldaten dead on the cobblestones, their Panzerfausts lying in the street in front of them. "Oh!" Joe exclaimed. "Good work, Shorty! Okay, let's keep our eyes open. Where there are two there are probably more."

The fighting continued through the night. We had no way of knowing at the time what was happening with the other three task forces. In fact, the 32nd Armored Regiment was heavily engaged in the northeastern section of Dessau, which was also being bombarded with heavy artillery fire. It was there that the enemy's last reserves had been waiting. I nodded in my gunner's seat as vague scenes kept crisscrossing my mental screen, nothing specific, just scenes of men and tanks and smoke and casualties and endless streams of surrendering Germans, trudging in defeat. Then I was asleep.

Before daylight we were called back into action to help repulse a German counterattack near the center of the city. It was a last-ditch, do-or-die action, and the fighting was intense. Pete thought we still had ammo enough to get us through. Tired as we were, we had to focus on what we were doing. It wasn't easy.

A panzer spotted us and let go with his 88. The round was low and passed under our tank belly, between the tracks.

"Hit 'im, gunner!" Joe yelled into the intercom.

I fired at him and glanced a round off the side of his turret. Joe ordered Graver to maneuver us out of their range. But then a second panzer appeared on the next street. Graver managed to get us around the corner and behind a factory building before they could hit us. At the back of the factory, he saw an entrance to the building set back from the road, a narrow inset in the building itself. He backed the tank into this entranceway, but not so far that we didn't have a good view of the road. We were in place when the first of the two panzers moved slowly into view from the right.

"Wait till you have a dead shot," said Joe. "They haven't seen us yet."

As soon as the panzer was in full view, I fired at the drive sprocket. It looked like I shattered it. Before the gunner of the panzer could wind his turret around to fire, I hit him again, this time on the left sponson. We were rewarded with an explosive display as flames broke out.

At that moment, the second panzer rolled into view—they knew where we were. We had no place to go, so I prepared to fire again. But before I could hit the solenoid, the crew of this second panzer came out of their hatches, waving white cloths of surrender. They never tried to fire a shot! Joe waited to make sure they were unarmed, then climbed out of the turret and went to meet them. We watched as Joe and the German tank commander communicated. He came back to the tank and informed Captain Harkin about the surrender.

"They're not sure about what to do," Joe explained.

The captain's response was brief. "Tell them to do what all the other surrendering Germans are doing—give up and march with hands on their heads toward the west end of the city."

"Why did they give up without a fight?" I asked Joe.

"Seems they were out of ammunition, and out of enthusiasm for the Nazi cause. No more stomach for combat. They know it's over for them."

We were forced to hold our position, since our way was blocked by the panzers. Joe had asked the tank commander of the surrendering panzer to please move their tank, but for some reason he never did.

"Shorty," Joe called over the intercom, "do you think you could figure out how to move that tank?"

"Hell," said Shorty, "how hard can it be? Just hope I can get into the driver's hatch."

We watched Shorty waddle toward the panzer and climb onto the tank. He seemed to have trouble at first opening the hatch. Then we saw him crawl in. For several minutes we just waited while nothing happened. Suddenly, a burst of exhaust indicated that our assistant driver had figured out the panzer. He jerked it around a bit, but finally backed it out of the way as smoothly as if it were one of our own. We couldn't help cheering. Shorty waddled back matter-of-factly, as though it was something he did every day. And he waved off our "hero's welcome," growling, "Any damn fool could drive one of those traps."

The command came for Task Force Welborn to hold its position until further communication. It was April 22, and most of the fighting for Dessau was now restricted to the north, where the 32nd Armored Regiment and accompanying infantry were still engaged in intense fighting. The Germans were well positioned behind barricades. The end finally came following a massive frontal attack on the German defense line, which brought the Germans to their knees. This battle was over.

When news of the defeat was forwarded to the various commands, a great cheer went up from troops everywhere. When we got the word, we joined the cheering. Except for pockets of stubborn resistance in the city, Dessau had been taken. At last, exhausted and aching as we were, we could smile as we stood around our tank, smoking and talking. Pete had a big grin on his face as he came over to me and shook my hand.

"I guess the jitters paid off," he said, still shaking my hand. "Were we a team or what!"

"We were—are—a team," I emoted.

Shorty came over, and Pete shook his hand, too.

"We couldn't have done it without ya, Shorty," he smiled. "Where's Graver?"

"Ah'm here," came his voice from the driver's hatch. "Ah need a li'l celebration."

Graver came out with a bottle of cognac he had saved for now.

"Thought y'all might join me in a toast."

We passed the bottle around, and I felt the cognac warm my gut in a very pleasant way. Then Joe appeared from a discussion with one of his tank commander buddies, smoking his celebration cigar and looking pretty happy.

"Yo! Save me a shot of that juice!" he called.

There was just enough liquor to cheer us all. Joe looked at Graver with a wry smile.

"You sneaky son of a bitch," he said, laughing as he did so. "You had that goddamn bottle stashed away all the time, didn't you?"

"Yeah, but Ah didn't touch a drop of it until now!" Graver said defensively.

"I know," said Joe. "You're a good man, Graver. Without the booze you did a hell of a job."

The bottle empty, we felt pretty relaxed. I didn't notice my fatigue quite as much as I had, but suddenly I realized how hungry I was. I walked around the tank, looking for the battle scars I knew it must have. I saw a number of chinks and gouges in the heavy armor plate on the front and the turret. I doubted that a Sherman could have withstood that shell fire. It was the extra armor that had saved us.

We remained at the ready for the rest of the day. I ate some K rations and managed to get a nap sitting in the turret. My eyes burned and my head ached. I slept for an hour or so, and then woke up to the sound of many voices. Outside, several of the crews were gathered, swapping stories and smoking. Captain Harkin appeared and reminded the men that we were supposed to be at the ready. He complimented the crews on their excellent performance.

"One indication of a good fighting unit is how few men are lost," he said. "Our company lost three men—two wounded and one dead. Considering the heavy fighting, that's a hell of a record. We lost quite a few of our doughs, though I don't have the numbers yet."

On Tuesday, April 24, 1945, the battle of Dessau was officially over. Thousands of German prisoners were being loaded on trucks for their trip to prisoner compounds. This roundup took most of the day as the trucks ferried the prisoners to the rear. The war was over for them, and at last we could dare hope that it was over for us as well. We had no indication that we would be moving on toward Berlin. The Russians, it seemed, had been granted the dubious honor of taking Berlin, and we were told that some Russian units had reached the Elbe and were fraternizing with Americans troops.

The next day, the twenty-fifth, answered our uncertainties. The Allied front in the West was now stable. To our joy, we received word that the 3rd Armored Division was to be relieved by the 9th Infantry Division. This meant that we had completed our combat mission and would be pulling back.

"Where are we going?" I asked Joe.

"Damned if I know. Only thing I heard is that we would pull back to some temporary bivouac or something. After that, I suppose, it'll be the CBI."

CBI—China, Burma, India Theater of Operations!

"You don't think they'd really do that to us, do you?" I asked.

Joe and Pete laughed out loud at my naïveté.

"Why do ya think they have us?" Joe grinned. "Hell, they *own* us!"

My face gave away my concern at this bit of discouragement. Pete offered me some comfort.

"Don't sweat it! By the time they ship us back to the States, retrain us for jungle warfare, and ship us out again, the war will be finished there, too."

I prayed he was right.

Pete saw Lieutenant Wilson standing by one of the tanks, circling his arm for us to gather around.

"It looks like we're through here," the lieutenant said. "At 1300 hours, we're to be ready to roll. Gas and service your tanks. We'll be moving back to the vicinity of Sangerhausen. That's all the information I have at present. Any questions?"

One question: "Are we on our way home?"

The lieutenant knitted his brow and said, "Wish I could give a positive on that, but I've had no word. Sorry."

At 1300 hours, the 3rd Armored Division began the trek back over the road we had traveled to get here, our tank cannons secured over the back decks. In this case, the gun barrel was faced toward the back and locked in a ring-mount. No need to be battle-ready now. The Germans had given up. And the evidence of their defeat littered the fields and the roadside as we went. Not all of the litter was German, of course. There were Shermans and half-tracks among the debris, reminders that our road had not been an easy one. I rode on the back deck with Joe and Pete. Shorty was driving while Graver snored in the assistant driver's seat. We had been moving for about an hour when the convoy halted. We were informed that we would be treated to hot showers.

Hot showers! Incredible!

The shower was a makeshift affair in the middle of a field. Here three canvas enclosures were each topped by a homemade watertank fed by large hoses reaching to a creek. Gasoline pumps brought the water to special tanks, which warmed the water with gas heaters, and thence to the watertanks on high. Yankee ingenuity had devised this technological wonder. The logistics, however, left something to be desired. The men were admitted in groups, twenty to a shower. GIs lined up and trudged naked through the ankle-deep mud around the showers. Once inside, they were given one minute to get wet—showers off—one minute to lather, if one could find a cake of soap in the muddy bath at his feet—one minute to rinse, after which it was outside into the chill to walk through the mud back to get dressed. No towels! Just cold air to dry us. Yet no one really complained. In fact, the mud provided a great opportunity for guys to engage in yet another battle. "Boys will be . . ."

CHAPTER 10

DESTINY AND

DISAPPOINTMENT

Our battalion was directed to a former SS camp in the vicinity of Sangerhausen, where we would have barracks to live in, bunks to sleep on, showers, and a mess hall, luxuries we had all but forgotten about. It mattered not a whit that the water was not very hot, the food hot but not very good, and the bunks bare planks—no mattresses. We showered in cool (but not cold) water, ate the food as though it were Mom's home cookin', and fell onto the bunks in our GI sleeping bags, straight into the arms of sweet oblivion.

No one woke us in the morning. Whenever we got up, we were directed to the mess hall for a breakfast of pancakes, Spam, and coffee. I don't think any of us realized how nearly dead we all were. We started coming back to life, however. For the first two days, we were pretty much allowed to rest and rehabilitate.

It was a very easy life to get used to, no regimentation other than keeping our barracks and ourselves clean—and shaven.

The SS camp was enclosed under a dense umbrella of trees, excellent cover for a military post. It was hard to tell whether the sun was shining or not when we got up in the morning. At the edge of the camp was a line of sheds under which we had parked the tanks. The half-tracks and other vehicles were lined up in a field facing the sheds. The camp comprised a large square a quarter of a mile on each side, lined with barracks, with a concrete pavement passing in front of the barracks. Along the north edge of the compound were the officers' quarters, mess hall, infirmary, supply shack, and so forth.

I really didn't mind when my name came up for guard duty among the first. Guard duty was limited to watching over the tanks and other motorized equipment. There was also a gasoline dump and an ammo dump included in the duty package. It wasn't tough duty, two hours on, four hours off, twenty-four hours each mount. Guard mount started at 1700 hours. I still had my grease gun, which, incidentally, I had never fired in combat. I'd found it lying in the mud in Espchenrode after our tank was knocked out. I wasn't sure if it would still shoot bullets—or anything else, for that matter.

None of the officers was available as duty officer, so a noncom filled in. Sergeant Meadows from Company D got the six of us who had guard duty together.

"Okay, look," he said quietly, "we're all pretty sick of the sight of tanks right now, but they've served us well. Okay! Ipstanowics [he mangled this one badly] and Firth—first trick. Irwin and Smedley—second, 1900 to 2100 hours. Rivera and Marchison— 2100 to 2300 hours. Then Ipstanowics and Firth and so on."

He looked at his watch, then at his duty roster, as though fishing for something military to say and finally settled for "Don't sleep at your post! Okay. That's it."

It was a wonderful guard mount, with not the slightest resemblance to those we had had to put up with at Fort Knox. No "Ten-*shut!*" or arms and uniform inspection, which would have been silly here. The four of us who were not on duty went our ways to await our shifts.

After only two days, we had fallen into a lovely routine of eating decent meals, playing a little soccer or badminton, doing a bit of untaxing guard duty, letter writing, and constructive loafing. German cooks had been hired for our mess, and local German laundry service was provided for our uncleanable uniforms and indescribable unmentionables. But we were promised an issue of fresh clothing "shortly," meaning sometime before we returned Stateside.

And then Second Lieutenant Shankers happened. No one had said anything to us about any new officers. But apparently no one had informed our battalion command, either. We were, nevertheless, favored with the addition of one of the U.S. Army's finest, Second Lieutenant Pollis Shankers, fresh from the States, no combat experience, his OCS commission not quite dry yet. Regular army. Best of recommendations. No previous command experience. (Gotta start somewhere!) Had requested "war zone" duty.

It was a chilly Tuesday morning, and at 0600 hours (an *extremely early* 0600 hours, as I recall), a piercing referee's whistle shrieked through the compound.

"Turn that fuckin' thing off!"—"Go fuck yourself!"—"Up your ass with that fuckin' whistle!"—"Go to hell!"—"Blow it out your ass!" These were some of the more courteous ejaculations that greeted the second lieutenant's signal.

"Five minutes!" came the official command. "Any man not out here and dressed in five minutes will be on report and subject to a company reprimand!"

It took close to twenty minutes before about thirty percent of the men stumbled out of their barracks to the parade ground in the central square.

Second Lieutenant Shankers stood with his hands on his hips, a fierce frown on his smooth-shaven face, outlandishly attired in spit-and-polished uniform—including a shiny gold bar—and glared at the men before him. It was his first view of them.

"Every one of you is a disgrace to the uniform of the United States Army!" he yelled. "Just look at you! Look at your uniforms! How can you call yourselves *soldiers*?"

"Oh, go shit in your hat and pull it down over your ears!" muttered a T4 from Company C.

The lieutenant walked over to him and glared into his eyes.

"I hope you didn't say what I think you said!" exclaimed Second Lieutenant Shankers with a snarl.

"Oh, for Christ's sake," growled the soldier, a veteran of four months of continuous combat. "The war's over—we're goin' home."

Lieutenant Shankers, outraged, cleared his throat.

"Your name, Soldier! Your name, rank, and serial number!" he roared.

The man stifled his anger.

"Lieutenant, I'm Sergeant Robert Johnson, 13593224. Am I a prisoner of war, sir?"

"You're on report, Sergeant. For disrespect to an officer of the United States Army!"

"Fuck you," muttered Sergeant Johnson under his breath.

"That, too, will be reported!" exclaimed the exasperated second louie. He turned to the private who held the clipboard. "Got that, Private?"

"Oh, yes, sir!" snapped the private, whose clipboard was completely blank.

Second Lieutenant Shankers then decided to deliver a lecture on military courtesy and discipline. He was outraged at the appearance, unmilitary attitude, and general laxity of the men before him. He assured us that that would change. He would tolerate no more such unmilitary behavior and no more disrespect to an officer of the United States Army. He expected each of us to shape up and live up to our uniforms and behave in a completely military manner.

"You are soldiers—*soldiers!*—representatives of your country. If you have an ounce of pride and patriotism, you will bear yourselves accordingly."

He paused and looked fiercely up and down the ranks.

"Have I made myself quite clear?" he shouted.

There was a PFC from Company C, a tall, skinny guy with black, straggly hair and bad skin, who decided that he needed clarification.

" 'Scuse me, sir," he called out, waving an arm toward Second Lieutenant Shankers like a school kid. "Are we back in basic trainin' or somethin'?"

The outburst of laughter echoed through the compound and lasted much longer than Second Lieutenant Shankers could have liked.

The Whistle again.

Quiet once more (except for snickers).

"I want you men to understand," snarled Second Lieutenant Shankers, "that you are one and all still in the Unated Stites—I mean, United States Army. At the moment, you are under my command. You will—"

The men could not restrain their laughter. It went on uncontrollably for over a minute.

Second Lieutenant Shankers stood silently before the men until the humiliating laughter finally died down.

The young officer faced the combat-weary troops and tried not to appear defeated. He was, after all, at the moment their superior officer, and they were still required *by law* to obey his commands. He calculated; he strategized; he redirected his thinking.

"I will detain you no longer at this time," he said quietly. "But the next time, I will exercise my authority as an officer of the United States Army. You may think you are somehow exempt from my authority, but I *assure* you, you are not. And I *will* use that authority to whatever length I must to teach you something about military courtesy and order!"

He stood glaring at us for several moments.

"DISMISSED!" he shouted and left.

He walked away with a swagger. The men broke up ranks and watched him in disbelief. It was an absurd performance, and no one knew what to make of it. They stood in small groups, discussing this new phenomenon that could hardly have been expected to boost morale. Gradually, they broke up and went to their barracks, most of them grumbling, some laughing. The mood seemed to have been one of dogged resignation—how long could it all last?

At 1200 hours, the piercing sound of The Whistle brought a new round of profanity, mostly stifled.

"Fall out!" came the commanding voice of Second Lieutenant Shankers. "On the double!"

They came out in various degrees of dress or undress, several with no boots on their feet. They formed an untidy cluster that vaguely resembled a line facing the young officer. This time Second Lieutenant Shankers presented a slightly more conciliatory attitude.

"I've been informed," he began slowly, "that you men have just returned from combat duty. That would explain your surly and unmilitary behavior."

He paused, looking up and down the non-line.

"I am willing to be patient, up to a point. It is, however, my duty as your drill officer to restructure your recalcitrant attitudes—"

"Drill officer?" yelped Corporal Benning from Company B.

Second Lieutenant Shankers walked over to him.

"This is an example of what I intend to eliminate. Private," he said, turning toward the man with the clipboard, "I want this man's name and serial number. And this time I will inspect what you have written down."

And so it was that this battalion was to be reeducated in the fine art of military discipline, including, we learned, *close-order drill!* It began at once. It may have been the most frustrating afternoon of Second Lieutenant Shankers's life. Doggedly, however, he pursued his purpose, listing every infraction, incident of disrespect, and item of insubordination, of which there were many. Most of the men attempted to go through the motions more or less correctly, but without zest. There was very little in their performance to cheer a military man's heart. At last, after half an hour of unsatisfactory "parade," we were dismissed.

Joe and Pete were already in the barracks when I got back. I shook my head.

"I can't stand much more of this chickenshit," I grumbled.

"Don't let it get to ya." Joe grinned. "Just enjoy it! It'll do ya good."

It suddenly dawned on me. Neither of them had been out there.

"How'd you guys escape the torture?" I asked.

They looked at each other, grinning.

"How's he gonna know whether you're there or not? He has no roster of names. Doesn't call roll," Pete said matter-of-factly.

But Pete had it wrong. Not only did Second Lieutenant Shankers have a roster of each of the companies, he had the Charge of Quarters post a duty roster on each of the bulletin boards the SS command had placed so conveniently about the compound. On the rosters were such duties as Area Policing, Latrine Orderly, Motor Pool, Guard Duty, Officers' Assistance, and a mysterious item called Watch. No one knew what that meant. In all the time I had been in Germany I had not heard such bitching as I heard from the clusters gathered at these duty rosters. The general consensus was that these "duties" were "pure chickenshit" and that this "chickenshit second louie" should "have his balls tied in a knot!"

Strangely, I rarely saw any of our own battalion officers about the compound. I hadn't seen Captain Harkin since we arrived. I began to worry about our predicament. *Were* we being retrained to go to the South Pacific? This new second louie did not fit in with our combat world—*ex*-combat world—at all. It seemed that our R&R was being transformed into something ominous, something almost surreal, something quite hateful. I felt morale falling all over the place.

At 1700 hours, Second Lieutenant Shankers held a Retreat, something I had not even thought about since leaving Fort Knox. I hadn't noticed the flagpole in the center of the compound with the new American flag waving from it. And, miracle of miracles, there was military music coming from a portable speaker by the flagpole. Bless his regimented heart! Second Lieutenant Shankers had acquired recorded *bugle calls* to go with the ceremony. All companies were called to attention as *Retreat* was played and the flag lowered by a sergeant and a private from one of the companies, all troops standing at "Present arms!" (but without the arms).

It was never clear to anyone what point there was to this sudden revival of extreme military regimen. A few days ago, these men were locked in a life-and-death struggle with Nazi madmen, going without sleep and food, watching death and destruction everywhere around them and fighting for their very lives. And now this. I decided to take a stroll around the whole compound just to see the place. Before this, I had taken no interest in it. I hadn't realized how large the area was, probably because of the trees. My walk brought me to the officers' quarters, a large residence containing numerous apartments. No wonder we hadn't seen our officers. I imagined that they were delighted to have some young duty officer stuck with "taking care" of the men.

By chance, someone came out of the officers' quarters just

then and I almost bumped into him. I suddenly realized who it was.

"Captain Harkin, sir," I exclaimed.

He smiled broadly at me.

"It's Major Harkin now," he said quietly. "My promotion has been pending for six months. Finally came through. Do you think it suits me?" He was wearing a green overseas cap with a shiny gold leaf on it.

Was this the infamous Captain Harkin who had shattered my military career not so long ago?

"It suits you fine, sir," I said. "You are a good commanding officer."

He chuckled lightly, keeping his eyes on me. "You know, when I first met you, Corporal, I honestly hoped I'd never see you again. But—and I mean this sincerely—your combat record is first class. I am glad you've been a part of my command."

I was flabbergasted and tongue-tied. Couldn't "sink" of what to "thay."

"How's that new lieutenant working out?" he asked in his usual direct manner.

"Oh, I don't think you want to hear about that!" I exclaimed.

He frowned. "Of course I do! I've been put in charge of him. How is he? Good? Bad? Half and half?"

I hesitated, not knowing how much I should say. I attempted to be discreet in my appraisal of Second Lieutenant Shankers. But I also wanted the major to understand that the men were not happy.

When I finished, he said, "Thank you, Corporal. Thanks for your candor. I appreciate your opinion."

I was barely finished with my little tour when I heard The Whistle.

"On the double!" shouted Second Lieutenant Shankers.

Once again the men more or less lined up.

"I have received orders to inform you, one and all, that henceforth there will be absolutely *no* fraternization with the enemy. None! Zero! That means: no friendly conversations with German civilians, no exchanging or bartering of any kind. You are not to give them such things as rations, equipment, fuel, food items, clothing—nothing." Second Lieutenant Shankers was at his most officious in this presentation.

One of the men—I couldn't see who—called out, "Hey, Lieutenant, can we kiss 'em if we don't talk to 'em?"

At that moment, I noticed Major Harkin approaching to the rear of the lieutenant. It was not a good moment for Second Lieutenant Shankers to lose his temper. But he did. He went to the part of the line where the voice had come from, and in an enraged voice ordered "whoever had made that remark" to come forward. No one did, of course. Without waiting any longer, he ordered the entire collection of men to "ten-*shut!*" then to "right face," and to "forward march."

"Hup! Hup! Hup!" called the lieutenant.

"Hup! Hup! Hup!" mimicked someone loudly and out of cadence.

Before the young officer could do another thing, Major Harkin came over behind him and cleared his throat. The lieutenant looked around, saluted, and the major returned the salute.

"May I have a word with you, Lieutenant?" he asked quietly.

Second Lieutenant Shankers called the men to "Halt!" He and the major then started to walk away together. They stopped, and the major called, "At ease, men. Fall out!"

For some wonderful reason, we never saw or heard of Second Lieutenant Shankers again. His assignment, it seems, was someone's boner in headquarters, someone who had a vague idea of what sort of creature Second Lieutenant Shankers was but no idea of what to do with him. Whatever the final disposition of Second Lieutenant Pollis Shankers was, at least we didn't have to know about it.

"What's this stuff about fraternizing?" I asked Joe, figuring Joe knew everything.

He shrugged. "No idea! First time I ever heard of it."

Graver, who was not assigned to our barracks, came in looking a bit shaky, so I figured he was hunting for booze somewhere.

"Hey, Graver," called Pete, "what do you know about this fraternization ban?"

Graver seemed to have good connections in the rumor mill.

"It's true. No fraternizing with the Germans. Ah hear there's a sixty-four dollar fine if you get caught. Anyone got something to drink?"

"Oh," said Joe, "too cheap to pay sixty-four dollars for something to drink, eh?"

Sixty-four dollars was more than I earned in a month. But I couldn't figure out what the problem was.

"Why're they doing this?" I asked.

Nobody seemed to know. Must be a problem somewhere. In time we found out that in some areas GIs were bartering army property, including food, PX rations, clothing, and the like— even gasoline—with the German fräuleins in exchange for the loving relations they were not getting from their wives or girl-friends. The term "fraternizing" quickly became synonymous with "shacking up." (Ultimately, both of these notions were neatly covered by "spazieren," literally, "to take a walk." "Hey, Frawlein! Du gay spazieren mit me?" GIs were marvelous linguists—as long as sex or booze were involved.)

I volunteered for guard duty just to give my life some purpose. R&R was a blessed antidote to those interminable weeks of com-bat, but I was beginning to feel ready to live again. That meant that I needed to have something definite to do. So guard duty, which made little actual demand on a man, seemed like the right way to go. I was on the second shift, which put me on duty from one to three on Tuesday afternoon. It was a warm, sunny day in May, and I was smoking and basking and rejoicing that the world was such a pleasant place. I was leaning against a tank, my eyes closed, daydreaming that I was resisting the advances of Ruthie Collins, who desperately wanted me to take her in my arms . . .

Something took me out of my reverie and made me open my eyes. Not more than fifteen feet away, staring at me with huge, dark eyes, was a little girl, about five years old. She just stood there, staring at me between the straggly strands of dark brown hair dangling in her face. I blinked several times to make sure I was back from my reverie. I smiled at her in my friendliest man-ner.

"Hi, there," I said, then tried to think of something I could say in German. "Uh . . . hast du ein Name?"

She just stared at me and said nothing.

"Let's see," I muttered, then tried, "Wo ist dein Haus?"

She turned and pointed in a direction behind her but made no sound.

A brilliant idea struck me. I reached in my pocket for the pack of Wrigley's Spearmint Gum I usually carried. I took out a stick and held it out to her.

She came over and grabbed it and hurried back. She opened it and started biting off tiny pieces and eating them.

"You're supposed to *chew* it, not swallow it," I told her gently, knowing full well she understood not one word.

"Uh . . . *chew!*" I repeated, demonstrating the chewing movements with my mouth.

She seemed to get the idea and started biting and chewing until the entire stick was in her mouth. Then for the first time, she smiled at me. It was all the gratitude I needed.

"Sprechen English?" I asked, for some dumb reason.

She shook her head.

"Sprechen Deutsch?"

Again she shook her head.

"Was du sprechen?" I asked in my hopelessly bad German.

She simply raised her shoulders, the international gesture for "I don't know." It occurred to me that she simply did not talk. Strange. What a sweet little child, I thought. Her dress was a bit faded and shabby but clean. She wore small boots with scuffed toes. I always enjoyed the company of kids, but this little girl completely disarmed me. Small children have a way of looking at adults in an unnerving manner, as though they can see things in you that even you don't know are there.

"Hast du eine momma?" I stumbled.

She nodded and continued to chew. She obviously enjoyed the gum. How I wished she could talk with me. Then I remembered my scout knife. I always had it with me—big blade, small blade, awl, and screwdriver—bottle opener combo. I pulled it out and showed it to her. She came over to me and studied it, watching me open the blades, one at a time. Then she held out her hand for it. I first showed her how sharp the blades were.

"Gotta be careful—oosh!" I said, simulating cutting myself.

She took the knife from me, studied it for a few minutes, and simply walked away with it. She had gone ten or fifteen steps when she turned and smiled broadly at me and gave a little wave. I smiled faintly and waved vaguely in return, not having the faintest idea of what to do. I wasn't *giving* her the knife, but she obviously thought I was. And I didn't have the heart to try to get it back from her. I was glad it made her happy, but I had had that knife since my days in the Boy Scouts, and I really did not want to part with it.

I watched the little girl go down the dirt lane leading away from the compound. I could not tell where she went. A small village perhaps, but it was some distance away. Well, I thought, that's the end of my scout knife. I lit a cigarette and went back to leaning against a tank. I went over the episode in my mind and got to wondering whether I was guilty of fraternizing with the enemy. Oh, but the only thing I had given away was my *own* property, not Uncle Sam's. Nerts!

Tuesday, May 8, 1945, was declared VE Day, though our battalion found out about it on Wednesday. It was a victorious feeling, if a bit anticlimactic for us. We had already been lulled into a postwar feeling. Nevertheless, that evening we were treated to a special meal, including real beef (not Spam), real mashed potatoes (not the dehydrated variety), gravy, green beans (canned, of course), fresh-made bread, real butter, coffee, and strawberry shortcake (minus only the strawberries) for dessert. And cognac! There was a great deal of cheer, laughter, and loud talking at the tables.

It was at this meal that Colonel Marsh, battalion second-in-command, addressed us and informed us that the men of the 3rd Armored Division would very soon be on their way home. That was as far as he got, for a tremendous cheer resounded so loudly that any Germans within earshot probably ran for cover. It was a moment of ecstasy. Graver was sitting next to me, and I actually hugged him, causing him to spill his coffee in his lap.

"Ah don't care!" he grinned. "Y'all can dump the whole blessed thing on me f'r all Ah care. Ah'm a-goin' HOME!"

That divine word "HOME" echoed from all parts of the mess hall. It was the reason we had all kept going. The conversations seemed to be focusing on what we'd do first when we got "in the front door." Things like: "The *second* thing I plan to do is take off my boots." "I'm gonna paper the bedroom ceiling with funny papers so my wife won't get too bored." "I plan to kiss all my kids, feed 'em sleeping pills, put 'em to bed, and hope they sleep for a week. That's how much time me and Jeannie'll be needin'." "First, I'm gonna eat a couple gallons of ice cream and a ton of hot dogs, and then I plan to get serious about eatin'."

After the racket quieted down somewhat, Colonel Marsh stood up again and continued.

"Now, men, I know how anxious y'all are to git home, but there's a sticker in the horse's ass. We goin' to have to put up with a point system. We can't all go home at the same time."

A huge groan swelled through the mess hall.

"Now, don't I know it!" he sympathized. "But that's how it's gotta be. We don't have many details yet, but it seems we all gonna get points for all sorts of things, like bein' in a combat zone—"

A great cheer, lasting nearly a minute.

"—the longer you been here, the sooner you go home."

Another cheer, not entirely unanimous.

"And you get points for bein' married—"

A loud whoop from the married men.

"—and points for each of your kiddies—"

Crescendo! Lots of daddies in this bunch.

"—points for each service star—"

Yeah!

"—points for yo' Purple Heart—"

"Yo!" "Whoopee!" "Worth *more* than a million dollars!"

"—points for yo' Good Conduct Medal, which most of you don' deserve—"

Lots of laughter.

"—an' points fo' bein' handsome, which *none* o' you gonna get!"

Colonel Marsh's Mississippi humor was the right touch for the occasion. While most men didn't know him, he was instantly popular. He could probably have run for president and these men would have elected him in a landslide.

It was a peak moment for all the combat veterans, a time that seemed almost to justify their months of misery. From here it was all downhill. There would be some anxiety until we learned how many points each of us was worth and how that related to the time of our departure.

On Thursday, May 10, the first of the high-point men received official notice of their redeployment to the States. It caused ju-bilation among them and disappointment for the others. Pete and Joe were both among those who got their notices. I envied them, but, in truth, I wasn't resentful. They deserved to go home. Not that I didn't, but I knew my short term, no matter how good it may have been, was not enough to put me up with them. But I did begin to resent some of those going home, especially when I saw a picture in *Stars and Stripes* of a train loaded with GIs going home. Plastered across the side of the train was a huge sign that read: FATHERS ON THEIR WAY HOME—OVER HERE LESS THAN A WEEK! My adolescent viewpoint was: "It isn't fair!" And I was outraged.

It was, of course, eminently fair that fathers should return to their families as soon as possible, whether combat vets or not. It would have been even better had they never been drafted in the first place. But it was a total war, and every resource of the nation had been brought into play. That meant that married men, even those with children, eventually had to enter the draft.

It was tough watching all the high-point guys packing and chattering about "release" and "freedom at last." While it didn't include Graver or me (Graver was just below the cut-off point, but way ahead of me), I was astonished to discover that it did include Shorty Irvin. Somehow I'd never pictured Shorty as a married man, and a father—of *three*, no less.

"Two boys and a girl," he said, with a grin. (I never knew he could grin, either.) "If ya ever get to Mauch Chunk, look me up. We'll go out and tie one on."

I took his extended hand and shook it. "Hope everything's okay when you get home, Shorty," I offered cautiously.

"It won't be!" exclaimed Shorty. "Wife's been shackin' with some asshole store clerk. I'm gonna take the kids and divorce the slut."

"Wow!" I exclaimed. "Sorry about that."

"Hell, don't be. I'm gonna enjoy makin' the bitch pay. Only good thing about 'er is I get points here for bein' married to 'er. And I'm thinking about shootin' the prick she's sleepin' with, the son of a bitch."

I guess I looked shocked.

"Aah! I won't do that. He ain't worth life in prison. But I'll find some way to mine his hole, believe me!"

I believed him.

Life is full of surprises, and army life seemed to present a grand assortment of them. I actually felt that I was going to miss Shorty. Never thought I'd feel that way. Yet one facet of military existence was the transient, serendipitous nature of acquaintances. Here today, gone tomorrow; close comrades now, strangers out of uniform. Men who fought together in foxholes or in tanks sometimes fail to notice each other on Main Street, where status and class differences once again mean something.

I volunteered again for guard duty just for something to do. I was starting to feel a bit empty. Somehow, standing guard was wholesome. It was necessary; no one wanted to do it; but to me it meant time alone to think things over and daydream. I tried to daydream about some more constructive things than girls. I had a future to consider, and now was the time to consider it. I hadn't finished high school, so that would have to come first. Then I would have to think about a job. I could go back to the Paoli car shop of the Pennsylvania Railroad, of course. The companies were required to rehire veterans to their old jobs. But I hoped to do something more than that with my life.

It was another nice afternoon as I stood my last guard shift, and I decided for some reason to take my dumb grease gun apart. Though I had never fired it, the barrel was really filthy; but I had no cleaning equipment. So I just screwed the barrel back on. And when I looked up, there in front of me was my little friend who now possessed my scout knife. And beside her was a woman, whom I took to be her mother. The woman held up my scout knife.

"This Messer . . . uh . . . knife yours?" she asked, smiling as she did so.

"Uh, yes," I admitted.

She frowned at me. "This no good thing for Kinder."

"No," I admitted. "It was a mistake."

" 'Mistake'?" she said, clearly not understanding.

"Uh—nicht gut, uh, mit ich," I struggled.

She understood. The little dear had *stolen* the knife. She started in on her, but I stopped her.

"Nein!" I said loudly. "It was a mistake."

"Ach, ein Irrtum," she exclaimed with an understanding smile. "Ah. So hier."

She handed me my knife, and I thanked her.

The whole time, the little girl looked at me with eyes expressing hurt. She did not understand. I had to think of something. Aha! The hard chocolate bar in my K ration. I fished it out and gave it to the girl. Her joy more than compensated for my embarrassment.

Her mother spoke to her quietly in German. She smiled and extended her hand. I shook it and understood for certain now that the child could not speak. Her mother sent her away. Then she spoke to me in the only English she knew.

"You good soldier. Me Tanya no having father. He killed by

Nazis." She made the gesture of shooting a rifle. I got the impression he was shot by a firing squad.

"Ach! Nichts gut," I said, feeling really sad. "Are you German?" I asked.

"Mich?" she responded, pointing to herself. "No. I be Ukraine. Me Tanya is me one Kind."

She was an attractive woman, black hair, pleasant smile and face, slight of build, and very feminine. She was the first DP I had actually met. Displaced persons were everywhere in Germany, most of them having been conscripted as slave laborers. This woman's husband had probably been a slave laborer who failed to please the sadistic Nazi guards. And little Tanya had no father. I smiled at the woman, feeling a tenderness for her. She came over to me, took my face in her two hands, and kissed me quite long and softly on my lips.

"Danke, Amerikaner," she whispered. "Danke für Alles."

She pressed a slip of paper into my hand, and then she left quickly. I stood in the aura of the moment, until I heard someone say, "I'm on now, Irwin."

Time to go off duty. But the glow of that warm kiss did not dissipate. I looked at the slip of paper. On it was written: "Ilya Yevchenko, Ludwigerstrasse 18."

"What do you make of this?" I asked my relief, Private Jenkins.

"Is that the woman who was just here?" he asked.

"Yeah. She kissed me," I told him.

He got a wry smile on his face.

"Looks like you're faced with the sixty-four-dollar question," he snickered.

"What's that?" I asked naïvely.

"You know, whether to fraternize or not. You go to this address and get caught . . ." He drew his forefinger across his neck. "Sixty-four bucks down the hole."

"Not this boy!" I exclaimed. "Not this close to going home. Here, you want it?" I held the slip of paper out to him.

"I can't afford it any more'n you can."

Still, it was the stuff that fantasies are made of. Romantic ideas—silly romantic ideas—stirred my virginal testosterone, and I dreamed of having my first sex with Tanya's mother.

When I got back to the barracks, five GIs were sitting on their bunks with their fully packed barracks bags beside them. They had all been re-outfitted—new uniforms, boots, underwear, field jackets—everything they needed.

"Hey, kid," shouted Joe as I entered. "Glad you got back before we left."

"You leaving so soon?" I asked.

"Soon as our taxi gets here. They said we were to leave by 1500 hours, but you know the army—hurry up and wait!"

"I wouldn't mind waiting if I could go with you," I told him, as I sat down on his bunk.

"Look, kid—Jack, isn't it?"

I nodded.

"Well, Jack, I wanted to tell you before I left that I'm damn glad you were my gunner. You did a hell of a job. I won't forget you. Try not to forget me."

"Wow! How could I? You taught me everything I know about combat."

"No," he snorted. "I didn't teach you a damn thing. You

learned it by yourself. Nobody teaches you about combat. Can't be done."

Even as we spoke, we could hear the trucks coming down the roadway into the camp. The command to "Fall out and mount up, all high-pointers leavin' on this train" brought a stumbling rush from all the barracks. About seventy men poured out and started loading barracks bags and themselves onto the two trucks. My envy index went through the roof as I saw them gleefully getting settled. I consoled myself with the thought that my turn would probably come next time. It was a good thing for my morale that I couldn't predict the future. It would be another fourteen months before my turn was to come.

I watched and waved as the trucks moved out, a feeling of loneliness washing over me. I couldn't help feeling a bit sorry for myself—maybe a whole lot sorry for myself. Then it occurred to me that I hadn't gotten Joe's home address. Shit!

ENDNOTE

Most combat veterans repress their memories of war chiefly because of the radical contrast between the world of combat and the ordinary civilian world they had been raised in and returned to. There is scarcely any way for a veteran to convey to his parents, his wife or sweetheart, his neighbors and friends, or the citizens he mingles with every day what he had experienced while he was away. The rules and values he had been raised with bear almost no relationship to the great killing machine called war. Likewise, the senseless demands of fighting and survival do not connect with the normal civilian world in peacetime.

Telling their stories is always difficult for these combat veterans and rarely brings them any social satisfaction. Even after more than half a century, recollections of personal combat of the fighting men of World War II can be painful to piece together. Yet there is always a cathartic value in recovering these dormant memories. These GIs were, after all, merely civilians dressed in uniform, most of them adolescents or not much older. It was never part of their brief training to prepare them mentally and morally for what they would encounter. That is what the veteran means when he says, "Combat can't be taught—ya gotta learn it for yourself."